# KALEB's FARMYARD TALES

## KALEB COOPER
### ILLUSTRATED BY TOM KNIGHT

First published in Great Britain in 2025 by Wren & Rook

ISBN: 978 1 5263 6776 1

1 3 5 7 9 10 8 6 4 2

Wren & Rook
An imprint of
Hachette Children's Group
Part of Hodder & Stoughton Limited
Carmelite House
50 Victoria Embankment
London EC4Y 0DZ

The authorised representative in the EEA is Hachette Ireland, 8 Castlecourt Centre, Dublin 15, D15 XTP3, Ireland (email: info@hbgi.ie).

An Hachette UK Company
www.hachette.co.uk
www.hachettechildrens.co.uk

Printed and bound in Great Britain by Clays Ltd, Elcograf S.p.A.

# KALEB'S FARMYARD TALES

# KALEB COOPER

ILLUSTRATED BY TOM KNIGHT

# CONTENTS

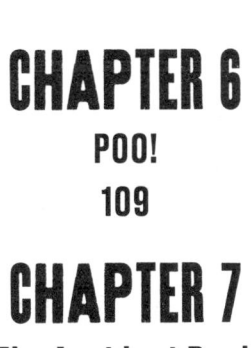

# CHAPTER 1

## MY FAMILY AND OUR ANIMALS

My name is Kaleb, and I am a farmer. I've been a farmer since I was a young boy, and I absolutely LOVE it. Farming is brilliant. I reckon that everything in the world can be broken up into two piles. Things that are brilliant, and things that are rubbish.

# Things that are
# BRILLIANT
## (in no particular order):

Farming

Tractors

My family

My dog

Cows

Chickens

Pigs

Manchester United

Poached eggs on toast

New haircuts

# Things that are
## RUBBISH
(also in no particular order):

Cities

Rabbits

City people who come to live in
the country

Jeff the Mad Rooster

Sheep

Tea and biscuits

You might have noticed that the rubbish list is much shorter than the brilliant list, which is how it should be. As you read on, I'll explain more about why I think the good things are good and the bad things are bad. For now, let me introduce myself and my family.

I live slap bang in the middle of England with my fiancée, Taya, our two children, Oscar and Willa, and our dog, Alfie. Alfie is a Labrador. Labradors are hunting dogs and their job is to bring back birds like pheasants and whatnot. I think hunting is cruel, so Alfie doesn't have much of a job to do. He spends his time staring at tennis balls and sometimes **helpfully brings back escaped chickens**. He doesn't hurt them, but they don't like it much and they **squawk** and **squabble** and **flap** as he trots back across the yard.

Now, I don't have a farm of my own. I own a little patch of land where I keep my chickens, sheep, pigs and of course my tractors. Most of the farming I do is on other people's farms. I am what's known as a contractor. It's my dream to one day own my own farm. However, before I can buy my own farm, I need to work very hard.

# Dreams don't work unless you do!

Now, what else to tell you?

Oh, there's my brother Kieron. He'll appear from time to time in this book. He's a lot like me except not as good at farming. (Don't tell him I said that.) Kieron is good with cows and he's not a bad farmer, but he's never been quite as mad about the countryside and animals as me. When we were kids, he wanted to watch *SpongeBob SquarePants* when I wanted to watch nature documentaries with David Attenborough. We'd argue over the remote for ages until Grandad would come in and turn the channel over to a cowboy film.

So, what else do you need to know about me?

Well, I'm a farmer, and I wear farming clothes, which maybe aren't that interesting or stylish. However, there is one thing about my appearance that is **ALWAYS** interesting, if not always stylish.

# It's my hair.

I go to the hairdresser a **LOT**. I have the best hairdresser in the world. Her name is Jojo and she cuts my hair in her fancy salon. And when I say fancy salon, of course I mean a shed in her back garden. Jojo says I have great hair. Or at least I do for now. You see, my dad is completely bald. He doesn't have a single hair on his head. I know that one day I'll join him and become equally hairless up on top. So I'm determined to try every haircut in the world before that happens.

I've had a **topknot**, a **Mohawk** and a **skin fade**. I've tried the **seagull** and the **mullet**. I've had a **buzz cut**, a **crew cut** and a **bowl cut**. I'm even looking forward to trying the **comb-over** when my hair does start to go.

You know what a comb-over is, don't you? It's when the hair on the top has gone so you grow your hair on the side of your head long and sort of fold it over the top. Some people think comb-overs look rubbish, but I say, why not? **If you've got it, flaunt it.**

I think my favourite hairstyle I've ever had was a perm, which is short for permanent wave. As I was getting back into my tractor after getting it, admiring myself in the rear-view mirror, Jojo ran after me.

'Try not to mess it up,' she said. 'Don't wear a hat.'

'I thought it was permanent?' I said.

'It's permanent until you squash it,' she said, then went back inside.

So I didn't wear a hat for the next week even though it was the coldest February in ten years and I ended up catching a cold.

It was worth it, though. **My hair looked great!**

Apart from all that, there's not much else you need to know about me. Except that I'm a **TERRIBLE** singer. I once did a rap song in a cow shed and all the milk curdled.

Anyway, I'd like to tell you a few stories about what it's like being a farmer. Like I said, I love my job and my life, and I really hope you enjoy these stories and get an idea of why I love it so much. What I'm really passionate about is telling everyone about farming, about the countryside and about where our food comes from.

# Hint: food doesn't grow on shelves!

**Our story starts here** at home on a bright, cold autumn morning. We were having breakfast (poached eggs on toast) and Alfie was lying down in the living room, staring at his favourite tennis ball. He had to watch it very carefully in case it tried to get away.

'He loves that ball,' I said, shaking my head. 'He just can't stop staring at it.'

'Just like you staring at your tractor,' Taya said.

'I don't stare at my tractor,' I replied.

'You do,' Oscar said. 'You love your tractor.'

'That's true,' I admitted.

**'Maybe you should marry your tractor,'** Taya added. Oscar giggled at this. He was only three and he and his mum were already ganging up on me.

'I don't want to marry my tractor,' I said, patiently. 'It's just a machine.'

'I think you love that machine more than you love your family sometimes,' Taya said with a grin. Both kids giggled this time. They do like to take the mickey out of me. But they're right. I do love my tractor. Not more than I love my family, mind, but more than I love chips, or Manchester United, or even poached eggs on toast (just).

I use my tractor for everything. I take my nan shopping in it, I drive it down to the hairdresser, I drive it to my friend Jeremy's house to explain to him just how much better my tractor is than his.

Anyway, I was about to take another bite of my poached eggs when suddenly there was a huge crash from outside.

'**Oh no!**' I said. 'What was that?'

'Maybe the tractor has escaped and run off with the combine harvester,' Taya suggested.

I pulled on my wellies, and Alfie and I **rushed outside** to find out what was going on. I had wondered if it was best to leave Alfie behind, since this was not likely to be a pheasant-based problem on account of us not having any pheasants. And unless the noise had been an explosion in a tennis ball factory, Alfie was not going to be much help. But it's a bit hard to explain this to a Labrador who's desperate to go outside and get in trouble.

There are lots of loud noises around farms: roaring engines, clanking machinery, Jeff the Mad Rooster screaming his head off at four in the morning. But this had been more of a **SPLINTERING, CRUNCHING** sound. I was worried, because it was coming from the direction of the pig pen. Splintering and crunching noises are not good noises. **Especially when pigs are involved.**

Alfie and I ran around the corner of the barn and skidded to a stop as we saw the problem. The big heavy gate that keeps the pigs in was lying on the ground, all broken. Standing outside the pen, looking very pleased with himself, was **Bruce the Boar**.

Bruce had somehow managed to get his fat snout underneath the gate and flip it off its hinges. That had been the crunching sound. The splintering came when he tossed it to one side.

Now, let me tell you something about pigs. They are big, they are **heavy** and they are **very, very strong**. **You don't mess with pigs.** Especially boars, who are male pigs and are bigger and stronger than the female sows. Pigs are usually very friendly, but even a friendly pig can be dangerous, especially when they're the size of Bruce. They might not mean to hurt you, but they can if you're not careful. I reached out and grabbed Alfie by the collar. Alfie might have tried to 'fetch' Bruce, which would not have ended happily for Alfie.

'How did he break the gate?' Taya called. She was watching from the upstairs window, the kids peering out on either side of her. **Great, now I had an audience.**

'The pen can't have been strong enough,' she went on.

'Of course it was strong enough,' I said. 'I built it myself.'

'So why is it all broken and splintered?' Taya asked, reasonably. 'And why is Bruce standing on this side of it?'

**'Look, he's very big and strong ... and sometimes pigs want to break out!'**

I don't usually mind questions. Especially from the children. Like I mentioned, I love telling people about farming and where our food comes from and how everything works. **Questions are good.** Asking questions shows you're interested, that you care about the world you live in.

**But sometimes it's not the right time for questions.** And this was one of those times. This was pig-herding time! I told Alfie to wait. He's usually pretty good at doing what he's told, so he sat down, dropped his tennis ball and watched it intently.

Bruce looked at me.
I looked at Bruce.
I took a step towards him.
He snorted.

'Come on, Bruce,' I said. 'Let's get you back into your pen.' But Bruce did not want to go back in his pen.

**He'd had a taste of freedom and he wasn't going to let it go.** As I took another step towards him, he was off, like a fat pink rocket, across the yard, through the open gate into the paddock.

That's the other thing about pigs – they can run very fast when they want to.

**'What now?'** Taya called.

'This is a job for the tractor!' I replied.

If I had my way, every job would be a job for the tractor. I'm never happier than when I'm in my tractor, watching other farmers in the neighbouring fields, seeing the birds wheeling through the blue sky. I might be ploughing a field to break it up ready for planting seeds, or I might be cultivating, or drilling, or harvesting. Tractors are also useful for hammering in fence posts, or laying pipes underground, or pulling trailers around, or a dozen other jobs around the farm.

**I'd use my tractor to brush my teeth if I could only find the right attachment.**

And now I was going to find out if I could use the tractor to catch a pig. There was plenty of room in the cab for me and Alfie. We climbed up into the cab, then I shut the door, buckled in and went to turn the key in the ignition.

**'Where are my keys?'** I muttered. Alfie whined impatiently. We've been through this before. I don't have a great memory. I always hide my keys somewhere safe around the place (you know, for security?) but I can never remember where they are.

We had to have a bit of a hunt and eventually I found them under a brick in the barn. That's right, I remembered I'd put them there the night before so no tractor thieves could get them. It must have worked because the tractor was where I left it.

Then we got back in the cab and, with a roar, we were off, racing through the gate in hot pursuit of naughty Bruce.

Our house is surrounded by fields owned by other farmers, and they all have fences, or walls, or hedges around them to keep animals in. Or out. But Bruce didn't seem to know about that. The fences he broke down, the walls he jumped over, and the hedges he hopped might have not existed for all the good they did. He just ran through them like they weren't there.

I told you pigs were STRONG.

We drove across the field and saw a splintered fence with a **Bruce-shaped hole in it. Sigh.** That was something else I was going to have to fix, as well as the gate to the pen.

We roared towards it, but when I got through the gap in the fence, I stopped the tractor.

Alfie barked excitedly. He could see Bruce lumbering away from us, across the field. He looked at me and whined, wondering why I wasn't hammering after the boar. But I shook my head. Because Bruce had run right through a field of barley which was very nearly ready for me to harvest.

'If I chase him across,' I explained to Alfie. 'I'll damage all the plants. And they're not my plants either!'

It was true. I had planted this field, as it happened. But I didn't own it. Alfie cocked his head, puzzled. Alfie didn't care about plants.

'They're worth a lot of money!' I explained. 'Or they will be, when it's time to harvest.' Early autumn is a busy time for farming as that's when most of the harvesting takes place. It had been wet this year and everything was running late.

I tried to explain all this to Alfie, who was growing increasingly impatient. I'm not sure how much Alfie understands, but it's good to have someone to talk to when you're alone in the cab and I'll talk about farming to anyone who'll listen.

There are two types of farming. There's livestock, which is cows and sheep and escaped pigs and that sort of thing. And then there's arable, which means growing plants like potatoes, grain or fruit. Arable is much easier than livestock. You don't get potatoes breaking down fences and running off. Barley doesn't wake you up like a rooster 'screaming' at four in the morning. Fruit trees don't stand on your feet when you're picking apples. Arable makes the farmer more money too.

You might be wondering why we bother with animals at all. But that's an easy one to answer. It's because we love the way of life. And farm animals are an important part of that. They certainly keep things very ... **interesting!**

Alfie whined. He was right – it was time for me to make a decision. Bruce was getting away.

'We'll have to go around the margin,' I said, setting off along the edge of the field.

Alfie barked. I assumed this meant he wanted me to explain what a margin was and I was happy to oblige.

'Farmers leave a strip on all four sides of a field,' I explained as we bumped along. 'We use it to turn our farm vehicles when ploughing and to get all the way around like we're doing now. But it is also an area where we can grow wildflowers, which are good for insects and birds.'

Alfie seemed satisfied with my explanation and finally we made it around the field to where we'd seen Bruce burst through a hedge. We had to stop and open the gate to get the tractor through, which delayed us even more!

'We need to try and cut him off before he gets to the woods on top of the hill,' I said as we roared off again. 'Once he's in there, he'll be very hard to find. And there's no way I'll be able to fit the tractor in between the trees.'

**I hate it when you can't use a tractor to do a job.**

'Go, Kaleb, go!' Alfie barked as I revved the engine. The tractor raced up the hill, but Bruce had a good head start. It was going to be close!

'Nearly there, nearly there!' I hissed as we closed in on the boar. *He must be tired now*, I thought.

I had intended to overtake Bruce and steer him back down the hill, as though the tractor was the world's biggest sheepdog. But he must have heard us coming up behind, because just as we drew level with him, he put on a burst of speed and shot away from us.

**I almost thought I could hear him laughing!**

'Speed up!' Alfie barked. Well, I don't speak dog, but it was pretty obvious what he was saying.

**But it was too late.** Bruce burst through the undergrowth straight into the thick woods. I slammed on the brakes and we skidded to a halt just inches away from a big oak tree. **He'd escaped.**

'That's disappointing,' I said after a few moments. Alfie whined.

'At least I know where he is,' I said. 'I reckon he'll hide in there. There are loads of acorns for him to eat.

He's tired and he's not going anywhere. I can come back on the quad bike after I've fed the calves. Easy-peasy, lemon squeezy.'

Alfie looked at me doubtfully.

'**Trust me,**' I said as I turned the tractor around. '**I know EXACTLY what I'm doing.**'

# CHAPTER 2

## I HATE SHEEP!

Sometimes you have to make difficult decisions when you're a farmer. There's no room for being a big softy.

**Farm animals are NOT pets.**

So one day I made a hard decision. It was time to sell the sheep – mostly because sheep are rubbish, as I've already mentioned.

**Let me explain why sheep are rubbish.**

Those woolly so-and-sos might look sweet and fluffy and innocent with their big brown eyes. But they are a right pain in the neck.

Sheep spend **THEIR** whole lives trying to figure out how to make **MY** life as difficult as possible. If you put a flock of sheep in a field, they will immediately work out the **most difficult** and **dangerous** thing they can do in that field. If there's a low section of a dry stone wall, they'll find it and jump over it. If there's a wire fence, they'll get tangled in it. If there's something growing that makes them sick, they'll eat it. Then they'll be sick. Usually on me. There's always a boss who'll think it's her job to lead the rest of the flock into danger.

The boss of our little flock of sheep is called **Stumpy**.

We call her that because she never grew her horns properly. Oh, by the way, most lady sheep, or ewes, don't have horns. But our sheep are Hebrideans and they all have lovely long horns. All apart from Stumpy, that is.

So anyway, Stumpy's favourite thing to do was to jump over the wall and yell, **'Come on, girls!'** in sheep language. The rest of them would follow, then they'd all say, **'What now, boss?'** and Stumpy would do something **VERY DANGEROUS** and **NAUGHTY** like running out on to the road.

They had done this just the week before. We got a call from our neighbour and had to rush to catch them and get them back in their field. There was me, Alfie, Taya and my brother Kieron running after Stumpy and the girls, trying to get them to come back to the field. But no, they decided they'd rather run right at a lorry that was coming down the road at them at a hundred miles an hour.

We managed to stop the truck and round up the

flock. It took us ages, but we eventually got them back into the field. Job done, right?

**No.**

Because when we woke up the next day, they were all gone again! I had no idea how or where they'd gone. It was a good trick. Maybe they were all magicians? Ladies and gentlemen, roll up to see . . .

# the AMAZING Stumpy and her Invisible Flock!

Maybe they'd found a hole in the fence, or maybe they'd chewed their way through a hedge, or tunnelled under a wall using spoons. Maybe they'd all gone skydiving or gone off to London down the motorway, or maybe they'd stolen a car and gone to rob a bank or something.

Anything is possible when it comes to sheep.

We eventually found them stuck in the mud on the riverbank three fields away.

## Honestly.

The other thing about sheep is that they usually decide to have their babies in the winter or early spring and quite often in the middle of the night, so many times during lambing season you have to get up at two in the morning in the freezing cold to go and help them give birth to the little lambs. Even Jeff the Mad Rooster is asleep at that time. Sometimes I wake him up on my way to the lambing shed just to get my own back.

Oh, by the way, it's bad luck to look sheep in the eyes. **It gives them ideas.** You stare a sheep in the eye, you can bet they'll immediately do the most stupid thing you've ever heard of. **A completely new stupid thing that you could never have expected**, like leaping over a hegde, or burying themselves in sand, or trying to ride a penny farthing.

I promise I'll stop going on about how rubbish sheep are soon, but I've started now, so I'm going to finish because I want you to understand my pain.

Sheep are also incredibly mistrustful of me. **ME!** **Their friend and protector.** It doesn't matter that I feed them, water them, help them with lambing, and make them better when they get worms or other illnesses. They don't care that I'm the one who's always helping them out of mud pits, or disentangling them from fences, or pulling them out of wells. No, whenever they see me, they don't say, **'Look! Here comes that**

**nice Kaleb with some hay and an interesting new haircut.'** No, they scream in terror, run away from me and try to impale themselves on a fence pole. If it wasn't for idiots like me, the sheep species would definitely have died out thousands of years ago.

**You're welcome, Stumpy.**

Oh, and finally, the worst thing of all? They also like to fall over on their backs and then they can't get up. Literally, they just lie there waving their legs around like a turtle until you come and tip them back over.

I mean, how does that happen? Isn't that a design flaw? **Whoever built sheep did it on Friday afternoon in a rush.**

And one **MORE** final thing. These days, wool doesn't even make much money. The price you get for the fleece (which is the woolly coat you get from a sheep when you shear it) hardly even covers the cost of feeding the sheep and looking after it all year.

Like I said, sometimes when you're a farmer, you have to make tough choices. And sheep might be nice and cute, but they cause so much trouble that you end up spending too much of your time looking after them or chasing them down a busy road. And if you're not even making money from them, then what's the point?

So why do I have sheep, you might ask? Well, when I was young and foolish, I wanted to impress a girl. So I bought her a little orphaned lamb that she could cuddle and feed, because I knew she loved sheep, and back then I didn't realise how much trouble they were.

Anyway, that girl was Taya, and Taya loved the lamb, who she named Stumpy, and in time Stumpy grew up and had lambs of her own. And Taya must have thought my present was pretty good because she agreed to marry me and we had a few kids, just like Stumpy.

Well, not exactly like Stumpy. **Ours are a little less woolly, but just as cute.**

Stumpy's lambs grew up and **THEY** had lambs of **THEIR** own, and then before I knew it we had **EIGHT** sheep running around the farm. I was also helping my friend Jeremy with his sheep at the time. He had a lot of sheep and didn't know what he was doing. Those sheep of his were **even more stupid** than my sheep and they were really doing my head in. That was when I made the hard decision to sell mine.

So that was that. A lorry came to our farm and backed into the yard, beeping madly to warn us to stay out of the way. Kieron and I had the sheep in a little pen, waiting. The lorry driver put down his ramp and came round to help us herd the sheep into the back. We were selling them to a bigger sheep farm in the next county.

**Stumpy was last to go.** She looked at me as the other sheep went up the ramp, cocking her head to the side as if to ask me what was going on.

'Are you sure this is the right decision?' Kieron asked, with a frown.

'Yes, I am,' I said, firmly. 'They'll be happier there. Sheep are herd animals and the bigger the flock, the better, as far as they're concerned. Eight sheep is enough to be trouble, but not enough to be a proper flock.'

'If you say so,' Kieron said.

'Nice sheep, these,' the driver said as they trotted up the ramp, bleating away. I grunted in response.

'Don't you like sheep, then?' he asked.

'Don't get him started,' Kieron warned.

'Actually, sheep are my second favourite animal,' I said. Kieron looked surprised.

'What's your favourite?' the driver asked.

**'Every other animal is tied for first place,'** I said.

We closed the gate at the rear of the lorry, and I peered through a gap to see Stumpy looking back at me. She seemed a bit confused.

# 'WHAT ARE YOU DOING?!'

someone yelled from behind us. I spun around to see Taya running up to the lorry, looking cross. I hadn't told her I was selling the sheep. I didn't think she'd like the idea.

'Sorry, Taya,' I said, taking a deep breath. 'This is a business decision.'

'Open that door and let them out if you want what's best for **YOUR** wellbeing,' she growled.

'But Taya,' I began.

'But nothing,' she snapped back. I noticed Kieron had slunk off somewhere, leaving me to face the furious Taya alone. Kieron is always good at being somewhere else when there's trouble. Even the lorry driver looked scared as he got back in his cab.

I swallowed.

'Look,' I said. 'The sheep are so much work, and we don't make any money from them.'

## 'KALEB COOPER,
## YOU LET THOSE SHEEP OUT
# NOW!'

Taya yelled with such volume I nearly fell over.

I heard the lorry driver lock his cab door.

'They're not pets,' I said, limply.

'No,' Taya agreed. **'They are not pets. They are FAMILY!'**

'But, but, but...' I started to say.

'No buts, Kaleb Cooper,' she snapped. It was never good news when she said my full name. Then she went on. 'Stumpy was a present. From you to me. She has a name.'

'Well, maybe we can just keep Stumpy,' I suggested.

'Stumpy needs a flock,' Taya pointed out. I had to admit she was right, as I'd just said the same thing to Kieron.

I opened my mouth to argue, but I knew she had a point. Once you've given an animal a name, it's very hard to see it as just a way of making money. My shoulders slumped. **I was defeated.**

I could see the driver's nervous face looking at me in the lorry's wing mirror. I shrugged.

Then I opened the lorry and let the sheep come back down the ramp. I opened the gate to the holding pen and let them run free, back to their paddock.

**And as it turned out, it wasn't a hard decision after all.**

# CHAPTER 3

## THE ~~DINOSAURS~~ CHICKENS

Imagine a **fearsome, huge Tyrannosaurus rex**. It has **scaly skin, massive hind legs** and **tiny arms** that look like they couldn't pick up a football. It has a **huge tail** and **big sharp teeth**. Pretty scary, huh?

Then shrink that Tyrannosaurus rex down and down and down until it just comes up to your knees. Then **add some feathers**. Now **shrink the tail** so it's just a stub (let's add some feathers to the tail too – why not?). **Shrink those teeth** as well, while we're at it.

So, what do we have now?

# That's right, a chicken.

Not so scary any more, is it?

DINOSAUR ⟶

CHICKEN

At least that's what I told Oscar and Willa. I thought it might be a good idea to get them to help out with the chickens, collecting the eggs and making sure they have water and clean hay. **I LOVE chickens.** I started off my farming life with a flock of hens in my mum's backyard, selling the eggs to local shops and at the farmers' market.

I worked for a local farmer when I was twelve, doing the early morning milking. Mum could see I liked farming and loved animals. So she bought me three chickens for my birthday.

**I'd asked for an Xbox.**

I absolutely loved those chickens, though, and soon enough I had **450** of the squawking little things. And I was selling a LOT of eggs. Now, you might remember I said at the start that one of the things I do not like is tea and biscuits. Maybe that seems a strange thing not to like, but let me tell you a story and you'll understand.

I used to go round the village knocking on people's doors asking them if they wanted to buy a dozen eggs.

Sometimes they'd say no, and sometimes they'd say yes. And sometimes they were lonely and would ask if I wanted to come in for a cup of tea and a chat. Even then I didn't particularly like tea, but I have always liked to chat, so I'd always say yes. And the thing is, once you've had a cup of tea and a chat with someone, they are more likely to buy another dozen eggs the next week.

**It's all about connecting food with the local community.** Sure, you can get your eggs delivered in a truck right to your door, and they might even be cheaper if they come from a massive farm on the other side of the country. But a lot of people would rather get their eggs from the nice young man with the wellies and the interesting haircut who lives down the road. The fellow who comes and knocks on your door and has a nice chat and politely drinks the tea you just made him. **Especially older people.**

'Do you want a cup of tea?' they'd say. 'I've got some nice biscuits too.'

I'd think, *Hmm, I have to deliver a hundred eggs, get back for the milking in two hours, then home for tea, then do my homework and . . .*

*Oh, go on then.* I **ALWAYS** went in and had a cup of tea and a couple of biscuits.

**I drank a lot of tea and I ate a lot of biscuits**, but it was worth it. Because if you smile at someone, they might buy a dozen eggs from you once. If you sit and chat and tell them how good they are at making tea and choosing biscuits, then they'll buy a dozen eggs from you every week. **Besides, I like to chat too.**

Having said that, if I never drink another cup of tea, it'll be too soon. **And I'd rather eat a dozen raw eggs than half a rich tea biscuit.**

I was good at selling eggs. I never did that well at school – I always wanted to be out in the fields, or the park, or the garden. But I'm actually pretty good at maths. If a teacher asked me to add eight and two together, I'd just shrug my shoulders. But if I had eight cows and then you gave me two more cows, then I'd immediately know I had twelve cows.

**Just kidding. It's eleven.**

Wait. **No, ten.** I think?

Anyway, you get the idea.

I might not have been much good at school, but I always **WENT. EVERY** Friday.

You see, I was selling eggs to the teachers. I missed so much school that my mum regularly had to

56

pay a fine – £10 for every day I missed! So, she yelled at me, then I had an idea. I was making so much money from selling the eggs that I could afford to pay the fines for her. That way everyone's happy, right?

The school gets their fine, I get to keep selling eggs and Mum's not out of pocket.

Well, no, as it turns out. Because the headteacher found out and called us both in for a 'talk'.

'I'm not happy with this situation,' he said.

'Me neither,' I said. 'It's costing me £50 a week.'

All joking aside, an education is important, and I did go back to school and worked as hard as I could. After all, I needed to do it to get into agricultural college, because I wanted to be a **PROPER** farmer, not just an egg seller. And for that, I needed to know about cows and pigs and, yeah, even sheep. Not to mention crops like potatoes and barley and wheat. I needed to know how to drive a tractor and how to look after the farm machinery and how to fill out all the paperwork the government asks you for!

Education is important, and sometimes you have to be patient and knuckle down. So that's what I did. I decided the chickens could wait.

Anyway, the point is, chickens are generally pretty easy – even my friend Jeremy can handle chickens, and he's the **WORST** farmer I've ever seen.

Oh, by the way, a quick side note here: we also keep turkeys. I'm not as fond of turkeys as chickens. It's not that they're any trouble, really. They're just not very . . . permanent, if you get my drift. We think of them as guests who come to our place for a holiday. They arrive in the spring, we look after them for a few months, then they . . . leave. Just before Christmas.

It's best not to get too attached to turkeys.

## Anyway, back to the chickens.

The only problem with chickens was that the kids were a bit frightened of them. Taya seemed to think this was my fault.

'Maybe you shouldn't have told them the chickens were dinosaurs,' she suggested.

**'LITTLE dinosaurs,'** I said. 'I told them they were little dinosaurs. **With feathers.'**

'Dinosaurs are terrifying,' Taya pointed out. 'Even little ones with feathers.'

'The kids LOVE dinosaurs,' I protested. 'They watch programmes about dinosaurs all the time!'

'They watch *Terry's Dino Club*,' Taya told me. 'Happy fluffy dinosaurs with smiley faces and big eyelashes solving puzzles together.'

But after this false start, the kids gradually got used to the chickens and they were a big help to me and Taya – even little Willa with her tiny basket, carrying half a dozen eggs so carefully across the yard, a look of

intense concentration on her face. Oscar was already a **CHAMPION egg collector**. He's bigger and a lot more confident than Willa. Or at least, he was until **Jeff the Mad Rooster** took a dislike to him.

**Jeff is quite big.** Like most types of animals, the male chicken is bigger and more annoying than the female. As roosters don't lay eggs, they're not a lot of use except for waking everyone up at four in the morning. Generally, you only need one rooster, for breeding. So I think Jeff was a bit bored, and he decided to have some fun by terrorising poor Oscar. Oscar is bigger than Jeff, but not by much.

Jeff would sneak around by the chicken house, hiding away until he saw Oscar approaching with his collecting basket. Then suddenly, with a SCREAMING SQUAWK, or maybe a

SQUAWKING SCREAM **(I don't speak chicken)**, he'd appear as if from nowhere, launching himself at poor Oscar like a **feathery bullet**, **wings flapping** and **claws flailing**. The first time this happened, Oscar was taken by surprise and the two of them ended up on the ground, rolling about wrestling each other like WWC on the telly.

**It was quite funny, I have to admit.**

It's odd, because Jeff left Willa alone. I wonder if he thought she was just one of the hens. It's Oscar who was the threat in his tiny brain.

From then on, Oscar was more cautious. To his credit, he didn't give up on collecting eggs, but he'd wait and watch until he was sure Jeff wasn't around before **darting across the yard** to the chicken pen to get them.

**But Jeff was smarter than he looked.** He would wait around the corner of the chicken house for Oscar to go in, get the eggs, come out and head back towards the farmhouse.

**Then suddenly Jeff would POUNCE.**

The first time this happened, Oscar **screamed in terror** and threw the basket of eggs into the air before sprinting back to the house. That wasn't a great day.

'You lost ALL the eggs?' I said to Oscar, trying not to get cross. Taya gave me a look.

'We need to get rid of that bird,' she said.

'He has a name,' I pointed out. That turned out to be the wrong thing to say, judging by the look on Taya's face.

I didn't want to get rid of Jeff. He was pretty annoying, but we did need a rooster, and there was no guarantee that a different one would be any friendlier or might let us lie in until six in the morning. The new one might be an early riser and wake us at three.

Also, I thought it was good practice for the kids to get used to the animals, to learn about their habits and ways and that yes, sometimes farms could be scary places. You had to be careful and stay on your guard.

The next morning, I sat Oscar down and asked him

if he was OK to carry on with his job. He took a deep breath and nodded. **'Yep! In fact, I have a brilliant plan,'** he said. I grinned.

'He's a chip off the old block, all right,' I said to Taya.

'Yeah, he's stubborn,' she replied.

'You mean determined?' I asked.

'No,' she said. 'Stubborn.'

I watched Oscar from the upstairs window to see what his brilliant plan was. He walked hesitantly across the yard, clutching his basket tightly. Halfway across, Jeff appeared. **Oscar stopped.** They watched each other like gunslingers in a cowboy film. It was like Jeff sensed something was different, Oscar didn't seem scared of him.

# Jeff took a step forward.

# Oscar took a step forward.

Then Jeff screeched and raced towards his enemy.

I thought Oscar would cut and run at that point.

Honestly, I think I would have. Jeff can look pretty

scary, even if he's not a dinosaur.

But **Oscar didn't run**. Instead, he reached into his

pocket and pulled out a handful of sweetcorn. He flung

it to his right. **Jeff stopped**, looked confused for a

second, then rushed for the corn, pecking like crazy.

All animals have two brains. One in their head.

**The other in their belly.** And in this case, the tummy brain won. Jeff likes causing trouble, but he likes corn better. Oscar slipped into the chicken house, got the eggs, refreshed the water and came out before Jeff had finished the corn. Oscar grinned then walked casually back across the yard, whistling.

'You know what?' I said later as we were having tea. **'That was a BRILLIANT plan.'**

'Thanks,' Oscar replied.

'And that's given me an idea about how we can catch Bruce the Boar,' I said.

'Corn?'

'Well, maybe not corn, but food. His favourite food. We need to appeal to his belly brain.'

'His belly brain?' Taya asked.

'What's his favourite food?' Oscar asked.

I winked at him.

**'Apples.'**

# CHAPTER 4

## THE COWS

If chickens are basically just tiny dinosaurs, then cows are **MASSIVE cats**.

'What?' I hear you ask. 'Kaleb, have you finally lost what remained of your common sense?'

**And the answer is, yes.** But that's beside the point. Hear me out.

The thing about cats is that they all share some

characteristics. They all sleep a lot. When they're not sleeping, they usually just sit there staring at you. They don't like to be bothered and they simply won't be told what to do.

There's a law that says if your dog causes trouble, it's your fault because you're supposed to be keeping your dog under control. But if your cat causes trouble, then everyone just shrugs because what are you gonna do, right? **In the law, cats are considered free spirits.**

Well, cows are the same, at least in attitude. The only difference is that if your cow gets out of the field and causes a traffic jam on the busy B2061 road then the police don't just shrug and say, 'What are you gonna do? Free spirits, am I right?'

**No.** They get you out of bed at two in the morning to come and deal with the problem.

(Now, like I said at the start of the book, I don't

have a farm of my own, so when I talk about **MY** cows, I might be talking about cows I'm looking after for other farmers, or cows that I own which I keep on other people's fields. Sometimes I even graze my cows on what's known as common land, which is land that everyone owns together. **Confused?! Sorry, it's a bit complicated!** But basically there are a lot of farmers like me, who don't own lots of land but make a living mostly through working on other people's farms.)

Anyway, where was I . . . ? **Cows!** Like cows, cats

also have their own personalities. They're not all exactly the same. Some cats are friendlier than others. Some will follow you around and sit on you when you stop moving; others only come to say hello when it's dinner time. Some cats are naughty and full of the zoomies; other cats are calm and relaxed.

And that's the same with cows too. And bulls. One of them charged at me once and broke three of my ribs. Bulls can be really dangerous. But some cows can be really sweet. We have a cow called Chug who is just the **friendliest thing you've ever seen**. We called her Chug because when she was a calf, she'd stick her whole head in the milk pail and chug the milk down super-fast. **Chug has a bit of a sense of humour.** Like a cat, she'll just stand in the middle of the yard and not move, no matter how much you try to encourage her. You just have to wait for her little game to be over.

Then there's Heidi, a Highland cow. She looks really

sweet, but she doesn't take any nonsense. The thing about Heidi is that she doesn't like you looking at her. It's like she's saying, 'I know I'm gorgeous, but eyes down, buddy.' You have to look over, or to one side, or approach her backwards. Then she'll be lovely and co-operative. But if you look at her? Well then, good luck getting her into the milking parlour.

Different breeds tend to have different personalities, just like cats. Ginger cats and ginger cows can both be a bit feisty. I have an Angus cow who can be a bit wild. I haven't given her a name. She is definitely not a pet!

In any herd, there's always one cow who really loves you, and one cow who really hates you. Heidi the Highland cow is the one who loves me. The Angus-with-no-name is the one who hates me.

I also have Hereford cows, who are really slow and don't get a move on for anything. They'll go where you want them to go. But very much on their own timetable, like the X9 bus service from Chadlington to Chipping Norton. It doesn't make any difference even if you explain you're in a hurry to get back home and watch the Manchester United game. We also have Brown Swiss cows, who are even slower and are the stupidest animals I have ever come across – even dumber than the sheep. The good thing is they're too dumb to ever work out how to escape. I have nightmares that Stumpy will recruit the Brown Swiss cows into her flock and then we'd really all be in trouble.

I think my favourite breed of all, though, is the Friesian. They're the black and white dairy cows you might have seen in a farmer's field near you. A starter-pack cow. Friesians are very maternal and curious. When the bull knocked me over and broke my ribs, I was lying on the ground feeling sorry for myself, and a group of Friesians came over to check I was OK.

They **licked me** and **mooed in a concerned way**.
I grabbed one round the neck and used her to help me
get back on my feet.

# I LOVE Friesians.

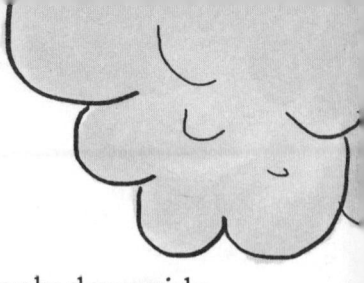

Friesians are really good milkers. The only downside is that I have to get up **SUPER** early to milk them. Not as early as Jeff the Mad Rooster wants me to get up, mind, but early enough.

I don't really like getting up early in the morning. Who does? But once I'm up and in my wellies in one of the milking parlours I work in, I'm in my happy place. It's warm in there. I can chat to the cows as I clean their teats and pop the little suckers over them. I play music and sing along (not too loudly, because as I said, my singing's so bad it can make the milk go a bit funny).

The cows do tend to fart a lot, if I'm honest. Cows fart out a gas called methane. Methane isn't good for the planet, but it doesn't smell of anything.

Cow farts also contain sulphur, which smells like rotten eggs, and ammonia, which smells like wee.

As I said, methane isn't good for the planet, and eggy-wee smells aren't good for me. There are ways to reduce methane gases from cows, including changing their diet and collecting their poo in big containers called anaerobic digesters, which capture the methane and store it so it can be used for heating or to produce electricity.

As for the eggy-wee gases – I just have to put up with those. You get used to it after a while.

During milking, the little suction cups squeeze and pull at the cows' teats, drawing out the milk, which runs along tubes into a big tank. When all the cows have been milked, a big truck comes and collects all the milk from the tank, then takes it off to the milk factory where it is treated to get rid of germs before it can be sold.

Did you know that a lot of people don't even know where milk comes from?

We get through loads of milk. Oscar guzzles it down and Taya has about fifty cups of tea a day with milk. Last week we'd run out, so I took the tractor down to the corner shop to grab some. There was a kid outside, and he looked up at my tractor with a grin on his face.

**'Are you a farmer?'** he asked. I nodded.

'Certainly am,' I said, patting the front tyre of my tractor.

'What sort of farmer?'

'All sorts,' I replied. 'Been milking the cows this morning.'

He looked confused.

'Do you know where milk comes from?' I asked.

'Of course,' he replied. **'Aisle 3 in big Tesco.'**

*What do they teach kids in school these days?*
I asked myself, shaking my head.

'Food doesn't grow on shelves,' I said.

'So where does milk come from?' he asked.

'From cows,' I explained. 'You put little nozzles on
their teats and they suck all the milk out from their
udders.'

'Then you drink it?' the kid asked, looking horrified.

'Well, no, not straight away. It's unpasteurised, so if
you drank it straight from the cow, you'd end up on the
toilet all day. It has to go to the milk factory
first to make sure it's safe to drink.'

'So, if you can't drink the milk
straight from your cows, where do
you get **YOUR** milk?' he asked.

**'Um, well, usually aisle 3 in big
Tesco,'** I admitted.

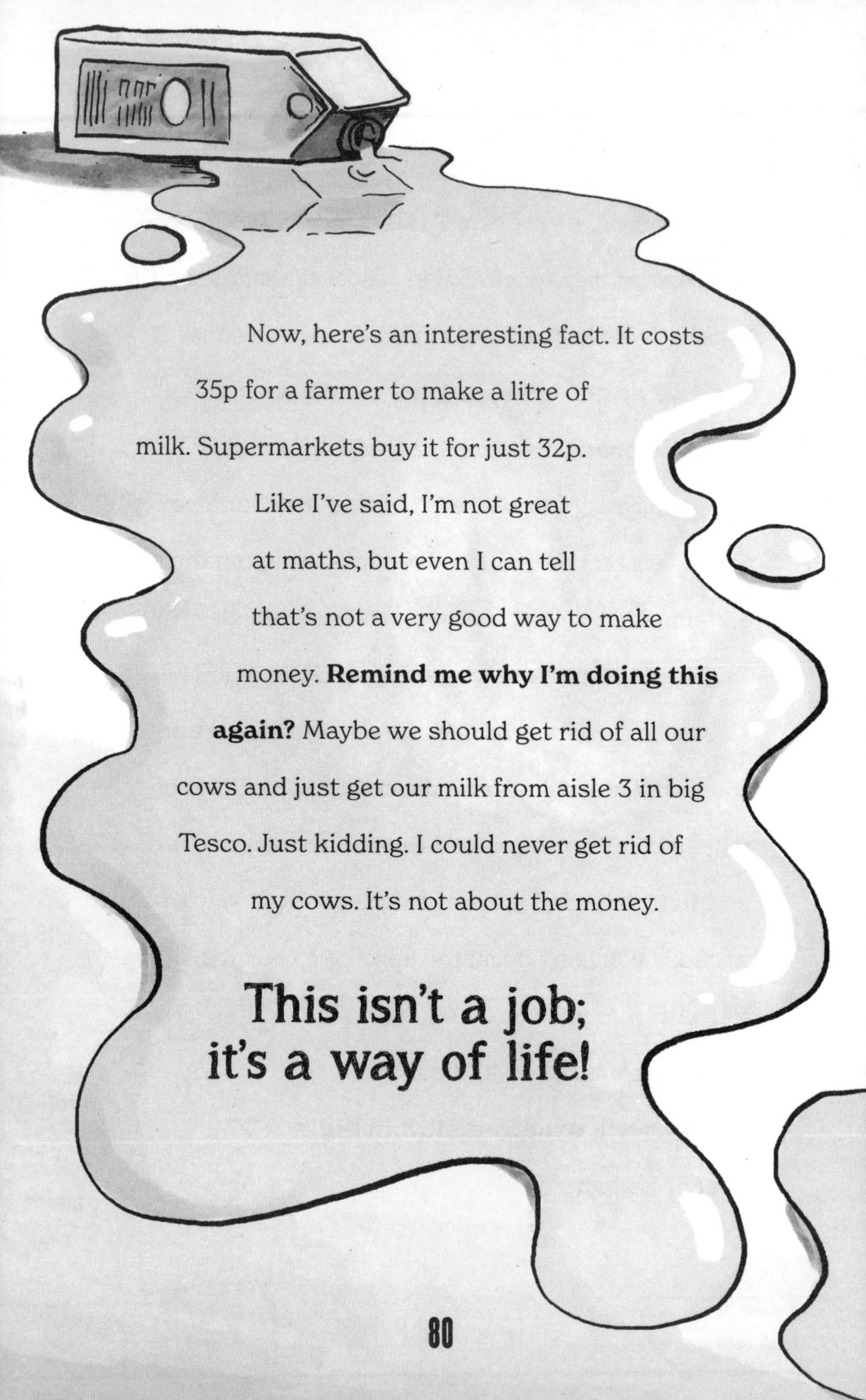

Now, here's an interesting fact. It costs 35p for a farmer to make a litre of milk. Supermarkets buy it for just 32p. Like I've said, I'm not great at maths, but even I can tell that's not a very good way to make money. **Remind me why I'm doing this again?** Maybe we should get rid of all our cows and just get our milk from aisle 3 in big Tesco. Just kidding. I could never get rid of my cows. It's not about the money.

## This isn't a job; it's a way of life!

Cows are great, but they can be hard work. Cats sort of look after themselves. Like I said, they're free spirits. And that's where they are most different to cows.

Usually when I get a call in the middle of the night telling me one of my animals has escaped and is causing havoc somewhere, it's a neighbour or a police officer. But this time the call came from the vicar of the local church. **So that made a nice change, I suppose.**

This vicar called at two in the morning to tell me Chug had somehow got out of her field and was wandering around the churchyard. Like I said, cows are **NOT** free spirits in the eyes of the law, and they're also not free spirits in the eyes of the local vicar. Any trouble caused by Chug that night was going to be **entirely my fault**. Fair enough.

So I got out of bed and pulled on my trousers.

'Where are you going?' Taya asked, sleepily.

'I'm going to church,' I said.

'OK,' she said and went back to sleep.

I found Chug standing in the middle of the graveyard around the back of the church. **What on earth was she doing here?**

In the glare from my car headlights, it looked like she was delighted to see me. *You're here too!* she seemed to be thinking. *Isn't this great?!* Alfie was scampering around too, also super excited by these late-night shenanigans.

'We're not having a party here, guys,' I sighed. 'Can everyone calm down?'

I walked over to Chug. 'Come on, you,' I said. 'Fun's over, let's get back home.'

But Chug didn't want to go home. She was in cat mode again and did **NOT** want to be told what to do. I pulled at her horns, but she weighs almost a tonne and I might as well have been trying to drag a tractor with the brakes on.

For a minute I wondered about going to get the tractor and using that to push her along. But that might have hurt her. And I would have knocked over a dozen gravestones. I was already in trouble with the church – I didn't want a bunch of ghosts haunting me as well.

But I do hate it when you can't use a tractor for a job.

The vicar appeared. 'Hello, Kaleb. Thanks for coming down.'

'Sorry about this, Vicar. She doesn't want to move. You know, free spirits and all that?' I said, hopefully.

'Well, we can't leave her here,' he said, helpfully.

Do you know that in India, cows are sacred animals?

No one is allowed to touch them and especially not to hurt them. If a cow decides to lie down in the middle of the road, then that's that. Everyone has to sit there and wait for her to move.

See, just like cats. In fact, did you know that cats were worshipped as gods in ancient Egypt? So both cows **AND** cats are sacred animals.

But I wasn't in India or ancient Egypt, and I had to find a way to get this sacred animal back home.

'What are you going to do?' the vicar asked.

'I don't know,' I said. 'We could pray?'

'Hmm,' he said.

But then I had a better idea. I called Kieron, who was even less happy about being woken up in the middle of the night.

'It's not even my cow,' he pointed out.

But eventually he did turn up, and he and I, with a little help from the vicar, tried to push Chug towards the gate leading to the road.

Do you think it worked?

That's right, it did not work. I think you might be starting to see the pattern now. The farm gets an animal, the animal escapes and Kaleb has to get up in the middle of the night and has a complete nightmare trying to get it back in its pen. Meanwhile, everyone looks at Kaleb with a frown on their face. It's like they're saying, 'Call yourself a farmer? You can't even keep the animals on their farm. That's basically what farming is, Kaleb. Keeping animals on the farm. That's Farming 101. I thought you went to agricultural college?'

Then it came to me.

**'Yee-ha,'** I muttered.

'What?' the vicar asked. But Kieron knew what I was doing. He raised an eyebrow. 'Are you sure?'

I nodded. Then, quick as a flash, I ran towards Chug and leapt up on to her back. She mooed. I've been on loads of horses in my time. Kieron and I used to ride

a lot, pretending we were cowboys in the wild west.

**'Yee-ha!'** we'd scream at each other. **But this**

**was the first time I'd ridden a cow.**

Amazingly, Chug didn't seem to mind. Alfie barked excitedly and the vicar was shaking his head in astonishment.

**'Yee-ha!'** I yelled again and dug my spurs into Chug's flanks. Well, I bonked her sides with my wellies, but you get the idea.

And surprisingly, Chug started walking.

**'Giddy-up!'** I cried, and Chug broke into a trot. I steered her by using her horns and that worked a treat!

**'Well, now I've seen everything,'** the vicar said. **'It's a miracle.'**

'Now listen to me,' I said. **'I'm the sheriff in these here parts. I make the law, and the law says you're going back to your field, Chug.'**

I rode Chug triumphantly all the way back to her field and made sure she was properly secure this time. Kieron and the vicar went home to their beds. But before I did the same, I grabbed some long grass stalks, and Chug and I stood together, chewing on the grass, grinning at each other. Alfie lay nearby watching us, his long tongue flopping about.

## That had been some adventure, all right.

# CHAPTER 5

## FRUIT AND VEG

On the fields I farm we grow potatoes, oats and barley. We grow winter wheat and spring wheat. Those are the main crops around here and we grow those to sell.

On my land, we also have our own veggie patch where we grow food for ourselves. The kids like to help out with weeding and digging and picking at harvest time. We grow runner beans, carrots, soft fruit, onions and potatoes in the summer, and in the winter we grow cauliflower, sprouts and beetroot.

There's a strong fence around the veggie patch to keep the rabbits out. Rabbits are extremely cute but very annoying and destructive. Same for badgers. Badgers are a nightmare. They eat the crops, they can spread diseases to the cows and they destroy fences. They are wise and noble creatures and I could never ever hurt a badger, but if I came face to face with one, I would give it a good talking to, I can tell you.

We also have an orchard (an orchard is a load of fruit trees). We grow different varieties of apples and pears. We make fruit juice from the apples in autumn and we bake the pears and eat them with ice cream.

# Delicious!

It was autumn, so there were a lot of apples and pears waiting to be picked, and a lot had already fallen off and were just lying about under the trees. We always have more

than we need and it always

seems a real waste not to use them.

It isn't really a waste, though, because the

apples get pecked at by birds and hedgehogs

and then what's left gets eaten by

worms and rots down to provide

natural fertiliser for the soil.

But I had an idea for something else to do with

those extra apples. I chatted to Taya about it over

breakfast a few days after Bruce escaped. My

neighbour had spotted him on his land a few times

but we hadn't been able to tempt him back to his

pen. But Oscar's clever plan to distract Jeff with

some tasty corn had given me an idea.

'Why on earth would Bruce want to escape?' I

asked Taya, shaking my head as I munched.

'Don't speak with your mouth full,' she said.

I chewed quickly and repeated the question.

'I mean, he has a nice warm pen,' I went on. 'He has his sows and piglets to keep him company. He has nice clean mud to roll around in and a lovely view over the fields, and regular food delivered to his door like I'm Deliveroo. It's unbelievable.'

'I don't think it's unbelievable,' Taya said. 'He wants to get out, away from his pen, and see the outside world.'

'Where's he going to go? Banbury? Cheltenham?' I asked. 'Or London? **Is he going to take the Eurostar to Paris?'**

'It'd be nice if **SOMEONE** got to go to Paris,' Taya sighed.

'Why would anyone want to leave this area?' I went on, genuinely puzzled. 'Why would anyone want to see the outside world? Farms are the best thing ever. The outside world is full of cars and buildings and aeroplanes and people I don't know.'

'You know that there are farms in other parts of the world, right?' Taya asked.

'Yes, of course.'

'And wouldn't you like to see those farms?'

'Well, yes,' I said. It was true. I love the idea of seeing how they farm rice in Thailand, or herd reindeer in Finland.

'And didn't you always want to go to America and ride a horse?' Taya said. 'That's what Kieron told me.'

'Well, maybe,' I said, though now I knew I could ride Chug that didn't seem so important.

'And you know that in order to go to America,' Taya went on. 'You would have to leave this place?'

'Well, that's the bit I'm not happy about,' I said as I munched on my poached eggs and toast. Alfie had added to his ball collection and now was protecting three tennis balls and two cricket balls.

'And you know you'd have to travel?' Taya asked. 'To get to any of those countries, you'd have to fly in a plane.'

'Hmm,' I said. It was sounding less and less appealing.

'Wouldn't you like to get on a plane?' Taya asked. She had a dreamy look in her eye I wasn't too happy about.

'Look, never mind about that,' I said, not liking where this was heading. 'Who's going to help me pick some apples?'

The plan was to pick loads of Bruce's **FAVOURITE** apples (Golden Delicious) then leave them in a row leading to the pen. I'd already mentioned it to the farmer who owned the woods and he was fine with my master plan.

**'Like the trail of breadcrumbs in *Hansel and Gretel*,'** I said.

'I don't think that worked out for them,' Taya said. 'They got captured by a witch.'

'It'll work this time,' I said, impatiently. 'He'll gobble them up one by one, and without noticing, he'll take himself home. All we'd have to do is close the gate behind him.'

'What could possibly go wrong?' Taya asked.

'Absolutely nothing,' I said. 'And the best thing about it? I can use the tractor!'

'Tractor,' Willa said. I think 'tractor' was her first word. Taya says it was 'mama' but I don't remember it that way.

**'Now, where are my keys?'** I asked, patting my pockets. There was a brief pause while we all ran around looking for my tractor keys. **Taya eventually found them in the fridge.**

It was a Saturday, so I took Oscar and Alfie with me in the tractor cab. They'd be safe in there. Willa was still a bit too little for this sort of thing, but it wouldn't be long before she'd be able to come with us.

We roared up the hill and Oscar and I looked out at the beautiful countryside stretching away for miles and miles. It was a cold day, but the sky was perfectly blue. Perfect boar-catching weather. Oscar was grinning so hard. *He has the makings of a farmer*, I thought.

I don't know if I've mentioned this before, but there's no place I'd rather be than in the tractor. It's my happy place.

'See, this is why I love farming,' I said to Oscar and Alfie. 'It's hard work but look at the results!'

Oscar grinned and looked out over the scenery, but I'm not sure Alfie was convinced. There were no tennis balls out there in the fields and hedgerows.

It's a hard life, farming, and there's not much money in it. But we farmers do it because **we love the landscape**, the countryside and the open air. **We love our animals** (apart from sheep – although some farmers even love their sheep). And we **love the wild animals**, the birds in the hedgerows, the fish in the streams and even the foxes and rabbits. **They all play** their part in the balance of nature.

'**You know what, boys,**' I said. '**I'm living my dream.**'

Oscar nodded. Alfie looked thoughtful.

'**But DREAMS don't work unless YOU do,**' I added with a grin. This is something I say a lot. **And it's true.**

We stopped just before the tree line and I got out cautiously, leaving Alfie and Oscar in charge of the tractor.

Attached to the back of the tractor, I had a hopper. A hopper is basically a big bucket, with a hole at the bottom sealed by a plate which opens up at regular intervals as you drive along, each time dropping one apple (or one seed, or one potato, or whatever it is you're planting). You usually use it along with a plough. The plough blade cuts through the soil, and the hopper drops the apple/seed/potato into the freshly ploughed bit where it will take root. It's so you don't have to walk along with a big bucket, bending over and planting things by hand and breaking your back like they had to in the old days. It's also much faster, of course. And you can sit in the tractor cab, out of the cold, listening to the Rolling Stones at top volume.

# I love farm machinery.

I wasn't using the plough that day. I just wanted the apples dropped on to the ground, where Bruce would find and eat them, before moving on to the next one in the row. So the hopper was full of apples.

I grabbed a couple of the Golden Delicious fruit, **shiny**, **round** and **ripe**. I walked over to the woods and poked my head in between the thick branches.

'Bruce?' I called out. I immediately heard an answering grunt. I walked further into the wood and saw him on the other side of a small clearing. He was looking at me. I think he might even have been pleased to see me. Pigs often look like they're smiling, but it's a cheeky smile. Like they're up to something. But maybe he was genuinely pleased to see me.

*Maybe I won't need all the apples?* I thought. Maybe

he was bored and would just come along happily.

**Nope.**

As soon as I stepped towards him, he grunted, turned and ran off into a thicker part of the woods. His excited grunting almost sounded like he was saying, **'Chase me!'**

But I was too smart for that. I left the apples on the ground then walked back out to the tractor. I got some more apples and left them in a line back to the hopper, crushing a few to release the scent. I knew Bruce wouldn't be able to resist. They're called Golden Delicious for a reason. **They're golden.** Then I got back into the tractor, turned around and engaged the automatic planter function on the hopper.

And so we went, slowly down the hill, dropping apples at regular intervals. **This was bound to work!**

I had a few other jobs to do that day. I didn't want to go too far away from the pig pen because I wanted to be there when Bruce finally arrived. So I spent the morning cleaning the milking parlour. I shut the sows away in their individual pens, since the last thing I wanted was to trap Bruce only to have a dozen sows running around the place.

Oscar was hanging around too, watching what was going on. He was clinging to the gate of the pig pen, watching me. He had a funny look on his face. I could tell he was up to something.

I watched as Oscar stuck out his tongue and licked the gate.

**'DON'T LICK THE GATE,'** I cried, in despair.

**'Yum,'** he replied. Then he did it again.

Alfie barked. I looked up the hill and saw Bruce, the massive boar, come waddling down the hill, gobbling up apples as he went. He didn't look like he'd lost any weight up there in the woods. Acorns were clearly a close second to apples on the favourite food list.

'**The plan worked!**' I yelled. Oscar whooped and licked the gate again. I made Oscar go inside – to keep him safe from the unpredictable Bruce, but also to stop him from licking anything else. I shut Alfie away too, then I went back out and hid around the side of the shed. Bruce would carry on wolfing down apples, make his way into the pen, then I'd nip out and slam the gate shut.

**Everything worked just as I'd intended.** Bruce came into the yard, chomping apples greedily. If he'd realised where he was, he didn't let on. He marched up to the gate of the pen and looked ahead to where I'd left a lovely big pile of the very best apples. **What pig could resist?** I crept out carefully, silently, ready to charge forward and spring the trap as soon as he went into the pen.

# Then Bruce stopped.

**He turned around. And looked right at me.** *The clever fellow*, I thought.

We stood there, once again, like gunfighters in the wild west. Bruce grinned.

Then he did a **MASSIVE POO**, grunted loudly and charged off, back towards his beloved hill.

I watched him go for a minute or so before I spoke.

**'That's disappointing,'** I said.

# CHAPTER 6

## POO!

**Poo is great.** I really should go back to the start of this book and add the word poo to the list of things that are brilliant.

The thing about animal poo is that we can use it to improve the soil. Soil, or the dirt under your feet, is **INCREDIBLY** important. There's actually not much of it on our little planet and we have to be careful to protect what there is, because without it, there would be no crops, no animals and, eventually, no humans.

Soil is made up of tiny bits of rock, rotting plants and absolutely **trillions of tiny, tiny bacteria**, or microbes. They help by eating the plants and breaking them down until you get the healthy, dark earthy soil that we need to grow new plants.

But breaking down leaves and things is **sloooooow**. Do you know what can speed things up? **POO.** By which I mean the waste products of animals who eat plants. If you take a cow, for example, they could eat as much as 100 kg of grass in one day. A lot of that is water, and grass doesn't have much nutritional value in it. So the bits the cow doesn't need and poos out could be as much as **50 kg in a day**!

Think about how many billions of animals there have been on Planet Earth over millions of years. And just think that every day, every one of those animals has done at least one poo. That's a whole lot of poo that's built up over the years. I'm not good at doing maths and can't multiply billions by millions, but I reckon by now that surely the whole **PLANET** must be made of poo. **That's right, folks. We live on Planet Poo.**

Settle down now, because here comes the science bit. I learned this at agricultural college, so you have to learn it too. Cow poo, or manure, is also known as cow dung. It's mostly digested grass and maybe bits of grain, fruits or vegetables depending on what the cow has been eating. All of that poo is already partially broken down and digested by the cow's four stomachs (that's right, FOUR! Told you cows are amazing!) so it's brilliant for mixing with soil and making it fertile for more crops.

Cow manure is rich in nutrients like nitrogen, potassium and phosphorus, which are all great for helping plants grow. Manure is the right fertiliser for almost all types of plants and crops and it naturally makes the fields better.

Now, you can't put cow dung straight on to the fields because it contains a lot of ammonia, which we talked about before when I was in the milking shed. It smells a bit like wee. Also, there are sometimes dangerous germs in dung. So you have to let it age and rot a bit to break down the organic matter and eliminate the bad germs before the manure can be spread on the fields. It spreads like butter on toast. Anyway, one of the ways you can age your dung is in big containers called digesters, which trap the methane gas, which you can then use for cooking or heating. Methane gas isn't good for the planet so it's much better to use it for something useful! But you can also just let the dung sit in big piles for half a year. The dung heaps get very hot and that helps to kill the germs.

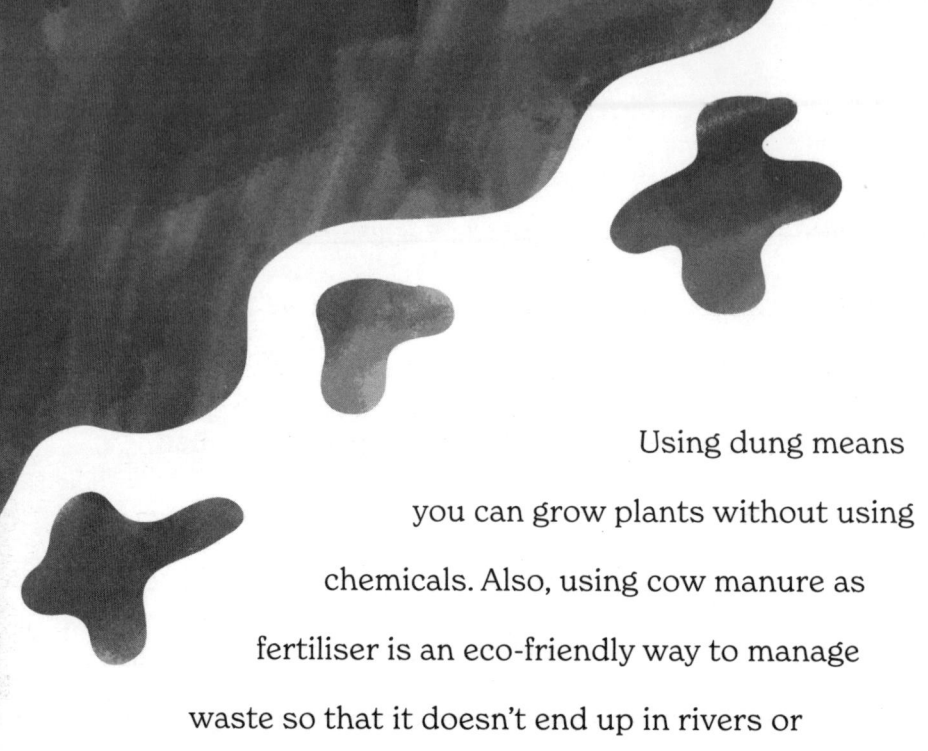

Using dung means you can grow plants without using chemicals. Also, using cow manure as fertiliser is an eco-friendly way to manage waste so that it doesn't end up in rivers or streams. **I mean, what else are you going to do with a MASSIVE pile of poo?**

One of the jobs I can do with my tractor is spray fertiliser over the fields, and that's one of my favourite jobs of all. It's fairly quick – the sprayer covers a wide area and it feels like I'm doing good. I'm super-charging the fertility of the fields and I'm putting life back into the tired soil, which works so hard to support us.

One time, I spread 65,000 tonnes of manure. That's right. **65,000 tonnes.**

That's 650 blue whales or over 5,000 double-decker buses!

**That's a whole lotta poo, baby!**

My grandad always used to say, **'Where there's muck, there's brass.'** That means where there's poo, there's **MONEY**!

Think about it. You take some cow poo, which is free. You leave it for a year or so (also free), then you spread it on your fields (quite hard work, but doesn't cost anything), then a few months later your plants have grown big and tall. **Bigger and taller than they would have done otherwise.** You don't need to buy chemicals. You can use the same field over and over, and you can sell the crops. So what's happened is, you've turned poo into money – something **NO ONE** wants has turned into something **EVERYONE** wants.

## That's pretty impressive, right?

The downside to poo is the smell. Spring is usually

when most farmers spray their fields with manure-based fertiliser and it can be quite a stinky time in the countryside. I don't mind the smell, really, because it makes me think of all the lovely plants which will be growing soon. And if putting up with a bit of a pong is the price to pay so we don't have to use lots of chemicals, then it's fine with me.

The kids don't like it much, though. And when I spread some good, well-seasoned muck on the veggie patch, they both started complaining about the stink.

'How do you expect Brussels sprouts to grow without a bit of poo?' I asked.

'Don't like Brussels sprouts,' Oscar pointed out.

'Good point,' I said. 'Neither do I.' We only grow them because Taya likes them.

I was about to give them an interesting lecture on the importance of dung when I heard a grunting and a rustling, and before I knew it, **Bruce the Boar came**

CRASHING **through the fence** we'd put up to protect the vegetables from the rabbits. He stopped for a moment, looking huge and triumphant. It was like he was saying, **'Ta-daaah!'**

Then he was running again, or, more accurately, charging, right past me and on through the veggie patch. He **knocked over the bean canes, ploughed up the carrots** and **ripped out three raspberry bushes**.

'Oi!' Oscar yelled.

Almost without thinking, I ran up behind the lumbering boar and was just about to leap on his back, like I had with Chug. Maybe I could ride him back to his pen? **After all, I'm the sheriff in these here parts**.

But pigs are not cows. Or horses, for that matter, and I knew Bruce wouldn't take kindly to being ridden.

I had seconds to decide – so I tried to get hold of him around the neck instead.

**But Bruce is** HUGE. He just shouldered me aside and sent me flying.

**Joke's on me, Bruce!**

I went sailing through the air and landed on my back. SPLAT. Luckily, the thing I landed on was soft. Unluckily, the thing I landed on was a big pile of manure, probably some of it provided by Bruce himself.

I know I said I didn't mind the smell of poo. But there are limits. And as I lay there, winded and watching Bruce crashing his way through the fence on the far side, I groaned.

'That's disappointing,' I said.

**'Do you still like poo?'** Oscar asked.

That's when I decided it was time for the local sheriff to catch that pig and put him behind bars where he belonged.

# CHAPTER 7

## THE ACCIDENT BOOK

Like I mentioned before, farms can be dangerous places. Whether it's being thrown by a pig into a pile of poo, or a bull cracking three of your ribs, or getting ill from licking a gate. There's always something that can hurt you. And when that happens, you have to write it in the accident book. **It's the law.**

Even if it's only a paper cut or a bang on the thumb when the hammer slips.

All the farms I work on have an accident book.

And, of course, you have to make sure you treat the injury straight away and write that in the book too – what action you took to fix it. I usually get a bag of frozen peas from the freezer and slap it on the injured part until it stops hurting. I use a bag of peas whatever the injury. Sore knee, broken elbow, even throat infections. I reckon we could save billions of pounds every year if they replaced half the hospitals with **gigantic freezers full of peas** and just told everyone to help themselves. **Maybe.**

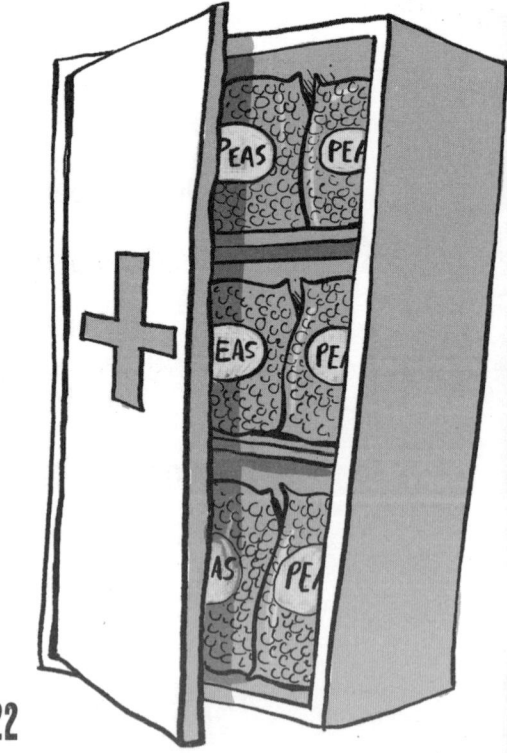

Our accident book would usually say something like this:

Name of injured person: Kaleb Cooper

Nature of injury: Cracked ribs

Cause of injury: BULL!

Treatment: Applied bag of frozen peas to affected area

Name of injured person: Kieron Cooper

Nature of injury: Sore thumb

Cause of injury: Bad aim with hammer

Treatment: Applied bag of frozen peas to affected area

**Name of injured person:** Kaleb Cooper

**Nature of injury:** Fertiliser in ear

**Cause of injury:** Thrown on to dung heap by massive pig

**Treatment:** Rinsed and cleaned and then applied bag of frozen peas to affected area

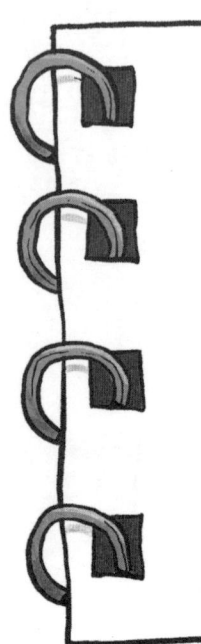

It might seem silly. But there's an important reason to keep this sort of record. If you have a big farm with lots of workers, then there might be lots of injuries. Unfortunately, some of them might even be quite serious. And if there's a record of all the injuries across all the 200,000 farms in the UK, then you can see patterns. What is the most dangerous thing? Why are these injuries happening? What can we do to reduce the number of injuries? **How much does a bag of frozen peas cost?**

There are a **LOT** of rules about running a farm, and it can be frustrating, but there's a reason behind every one of them. Sometimes these rules can seem a bit odd, like the time I had to strap myself into a machine that lifts people into the air, called a cherry picker, then when I got out, I forgot I was attached and the strap yanked me back so hard I fell over and bashed my head. But I suppose that's better than not being strapped in and falling off when the cherry picker is high in the air. I'd be hoping to land in a dung heap if **THAT** happened, I can tell you.

Now, I want to tell you a little bit about walking across farmers' fields. It's sometimes known as **rambling**. And people who do it are called **ramblers**. I think they're called that because they do like to ramble on about how great walking is. All over Britain, there are ancient paths that anyone is allowed to walk on. If you're ever in the country, you might see wooden poles with signs saying something like **'PUBLIC FOOTPATH'**, and there may be a yellow or blue arrow on them.

There are around 225,000 kilometres of public rights of way in Britain and most of them cross private land.

Because they are public rights of way, you are allowed to walk over them whenever you like. You can walk on them slowly or quickly, you can walk on them backwards or on your hands. If a big red-faced farmer comes up, waves a pitchfork and tells you to **'GET OFF MY LAND!'** you can ignore him and carry on.

But ramblers have to **respect the rules** and **be careful**, for their own safety and the safety of others. **Really, truly!**

For a start, you need to know that cows can be dangerous. Farmers aren't supposed to keep bulls in fields crossed by a right of way. But even cows can be dangerous just because they're **so BIG**. And if you get between a mother and her calf, then you might be in big trouble! As long as you're careful, though, and don't do anything silly, then it's safe to walk through fields with cows.

And **please**, **please**, **please** take your litter home with you. Crisp packets are not the best diet for sheep (who, remember, will eat anything that makes them sick).

There's another rule that **EVERYONE needs to know** when it comes to farms, and that is

# ALWAYS CLOSE THE GATE BEHIND YOU.

If you're walking across a farmer's land and you come to a gate, by all means open it and walk through, but then **PLEASE** close it behind you. You might find Bruce chasing you otherwise . . .

At least half the times our animals have got loose it's because some ramblers have left a gate open. Let me tell you a little story about the difficulties we farmers have with ramblers and gates.

One day last summer, right in the middle of rambling season, I was driving back from Jojo the hairdresser's in my tractor when I came across a herd of cows charging along the road, right towards me. *Not too unusual around here,* I thought. Often farmers move cows from one field to another along the road. But two things struck me as odd about this herd. Firstly, I couldn't see any people herding them along, and secondly, the cows themselves looked **very familiar**. I stopped the tractor. The cows stopped and looked back at me. I walked closer and realised why the cows looked familiar – **they were, in fact, MY cows**.

Someone had left the gate to their field open. I knew it wasn't me or anyone else who worked on that land. We've all spent so much time chasing animals around the countryside that we are incredibly careful when it comes to gates.

It seemed the cows had walked straight out of the field and carried on up the road. Cows are herd animals. They're not as mad as sheep, but if one of them starts walking along like she knows where she's going, then the rest will follow.

There were a lot of them, and I was on my own (though I suppose you're never alone when you're with a tractor). But I figured I could get them back in their field without too much trouble. The road we were on was long, narrow and straight. At the end of it you come up to the gate they'd come out of. There is a turning off to the left, mind, but cows tend to walk in a straight line mostly and I knew that if I herded them back along the road, they'd likely keep going through the gate and back into their field, especially when they saw all the lovely grass in there.

**'Come on, boss,'** I called to the lead cow, urging her to turn around and walk the other way. (I'm not sure why we call cows 'boss' – maybe it's because we secretly know that they're in charge?) She wasn't happy about it and mooed at me defiantly. Not sure where she thought she was going, except maybe to Jojo's to get a haircut?

Actually, that's not a bad idea. Cow Milking and Hairstyling Parlours – give your heifer a trim while she gives you her milk.

Maybe I could finally make some money out of the cow business.

**Anyway, back to the job at hand.**

Eventually I managed to get the lead cow to turn and walk back the other way, so the other cows decided she must have known what she was doing and they all turned to follow her. Luckily there was no other traffic on the road at that moment. There's not a lot down that road except more cows ...

Once they were moving, I got back in the tractor and followed them. We chugged along slowly and I started daydreaming about my cow hairdressing business.

## What could I call it?

## Moo Look?

## Kaleb's Klippers?

## The Hairstack?

Maybe I could do sheep too and call it a Baa-Baa

Shop. Then I remembered we give the sheep a haircut

twice a year anyway.

You can't hurry cows. They all just follow the one

in front and if you try to give the ones at the back a

hurry-up they tend to panic and start running around

in circles. I had a good view over the top of them from

my high tractor cab, and as we got close to the field they'd come out of, I peered over the top of them to make sure they were going where they were supposed to.

**That's when my heart sank.**

**The gate was closed.**

Clearly some well-meaning rambler had gone through the gate and decided to do what they thought was the right thing and close it behind them. I get where they were coming from but flipping 'eck! You can't win sometimes.

So this is the other most important rule about walking over farmers' land.

**1. If you open a gate, close it behind you.**

**2. If you see an open gate,**

# LEAVE IT OPEN!

**Trust me, we know what we're doing when it comes to gates.**

I watched the disaster unfold slowly. As the gate to the field was closed, the lead cow decided that I wanted her to turn left and carry on along the road. I can't fault her thinking on that one, to be fair.

**But what was I going to do now?** I had to get to the front of the herd and stop them again. But I couldn't very well charge through the herd on the tractor – I might panic them, or worse, injure them. I did the only thing I could. I let the whole herd turn left, then I hopped out of the tractor and opened the gate. I thought about writing a sign on it to say '**LEAVE OPEN, YOU NUMPTIES**' but I didn't have anything to write on, or with, if I'm honest.

So how I was going to get the cows to go back into the field? I could get ahead of them again and send them back again. But this time I needed them to turn left to go into the field, not right again and back to Jojo's for that haircut.

**So what have we learned about Kaleb?** If you have a job to do, find a way to use your **TRACTOR** to do it.

I blocked the right-hand turn with the tractor, then squeezed my way on foot through the herd to the front, being careful not to panic them. I'm a solid chap but being in the middle of thirty Friesians charging about would turn me into Kaleb paste pretty quickly. Finally I got to the front again and confronted the lead cow. She blinked at me in surprise. *You again?* she was clearly thinking. *What now?!*

**'Turn around, boss,'** I said.

She mooed loudly. 'Make up your mind!' I think she was saying.

But turn around she did, and eventually all the rest of the cows followed her. I held my breath as they got to the gate. Like I said, cows, like cats, won't be told, and I wouldn't put it past them to squeeze by the tractor and head off to Jojo's again.

But luckily they turned left this time.

Once they were all safely back in the field, I shut the gate firmly and breathed a huge sigh of relief.

A little beep of the horn told me someone was stuck behind the tractor and I hurried over to move it out of the way.

'Hello, Kaleb,' the driver said through the window.

'Hello, Jojo,' I said. 'Sorry about this. Just some trouble with the cows.'

'No problem,' she replied with a grin. 'I'm not in any hurry.'

'Oh, by the way,' I said to her. 'Have you ever given a cow a haircut?'

# CHAPTER 8

## CULTIVATION

OK, everyone, it's time for a geography lesson! Well, only a little one.

The eastern side of England tends to be a bit drier than the west. The drier conditions make it better for arable farming (growing plants), while the wetter west side is generally best for pastoral farming (raising livestock).

I live right in the middle of England. Which means it's good for both livestock AND crops.

Being in the middle has its good points and its bad points. Mostly to do with rain, as I just mentioned. There was a reason I didn't add rain to either the brilliant list or the rubbish list at the start of the book. Because it can be both.

Rain is brilliant when you need it, and rain is rubbish when you don't need it.

Think about it. Imagine your parents or guardians want you to come out with them on a long walk, to see an old building, or a garden, or some other boring thing. Then it starts raining and you can't go. Well, that's a time when rain is brilliant, right? You can stay inside and play games, or read a book, or watch telly, or start your own chicken business.

And then imagine you're going to have a barbecue in the park with all your favourite food and drink and

then you're going to play outdoor games with all your friends. Then it starts raining and the barbecue won't light. Not so great, right?

The main reason a lot of rain is a problem when growing crops is because you need it to be mostly dry when you prepare the soil, when you plant, when you spread fertiliser and when you harvest. Too much rain at the wrong time can make it hard to keep your harvested crops dry.

When it comes to livestock, rain doesn't matter so much. A lot of rain means a lot of grass to eat. A wet cow will still give milk. A muddy field is perfect for a pig, and sheep have thick woolly coats to keep them warm. (Though I suppose they must get really heavy when it rains?)

The year Bruce escaped, we had a really wet year. I mean really, really wet. Wetter than the North Sea.

It rained EVERY day for weeks.

And that was in the autumn, when we should have been in the tractor every day, harvesting the wheat, or the barley, or the oats. Instead I was sat at home, staring out the window day after day, wishing I could be in my tractor cab singing along to country and western songs and getting on with the business of harvesting the crops. If I wasn't in my tractor, I wasn't earning any money.

It was a miserable time, I can tell you. My grandad used to say, 'A dry year will hurt you; a wet year will ruin you.' And I thought about that saying every time I looked out of the window at the grey clouds and the muddy fields and the puddles in the yard.

And then one day I woke up and immediately noticed something was different. The bedroom was lighter. I couldn't hear the constant sound of rain bashing on the window.

I jumped out of bed and pulled

the curtains across.

# SUNSHINE!

**We were saved!**

'OI!' Taya called out. 'I'm trying to sleep!'

I pulled on my trousers and raced downstairs.

I stuffed a slice of toast into my mouth and Alfie and

I ran outside, heading straight for the tractor. I had my

hand on the door-handle when my phone rang.

**It was the police.** My heart sank.

'Kaleb? We've got some of your cows down here on

the road.'

I groaned. **Not now!**

I like cows, you know that. But just at that moment,

I wished there was no such thing as a cow. They'd been

on common land, but it was fenced, so they shouldn't

have been able to get out.

Could I just pretend they were someone else's cows and leave them to it?

**Not a chance.** The police know me, and they know my cows when they see them. There was nothing else for it – I had to go and get them. The cows were blocking the road and there was a great long traffic jam full of people trying to get to work and honking their horns. I had my work to do, but so did everyone else. It took me and Kieron over an hour to round the cows up and get them back to my land. We got a lot of dirty looks from the motorists, I can tell you. **But no one was more impatient than me.**

Anyway, we finally got them back home and chased them into the yard. I wanted them to go right across and into our field. It's not that big but I can keep animals there temporarily – the cows would be safely under lock and key until I'd got my ploughing done. Then I'd take a look at the common field to figure out how they'd escaped. Probably a broken fence or a tumble-down stone wall. I needed to fix that before I put them back there.

Only, today, the cows weren't in a very co-operative mood and they'd decided that as it was a nice sunny day they were going to carry on making my life as difficult as possible. Instead of going into the home field, they suddenly turned and charged in the opposite direction, right through the chicken coop!

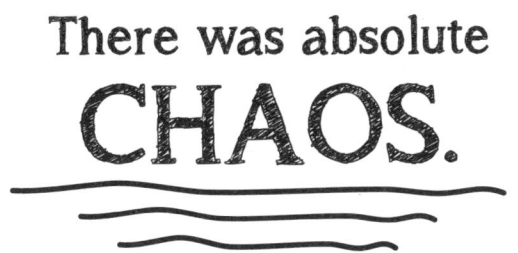

There was absolute CHAOS.

The chickens were **squawking** and

**flapping** as they got out of the way of this

terrifying stampede. Chicken houses were knocked

over, and the little fence we have to keep the foxes

out was torn right away from the posts and dragged

along by the lead cow. Jeff the Mad Rooster was **going**

**BANANAS**, screeching at me as if it was all my fault. Kieron was shouting words that aren't suitable for anyone. They even made **ME** blush, if I'm honest.

Alfie was no help whatsoever. In fact, he made matters worse by barking and chasing the chickens, snapping at them, having the time of his life. When the dust had settled, I surveyed the damage. Three of the four chicken houses were knocked over. The fence had been completely destroyed. The chickens were spread far and wide over the home field.

**'That's disappointing,'** I said.

The cows had decided they'd had enough fun for now and were calmly chomping on grass as if nothing had happened. I looked up at the bright, warm sun above. I could have ploughed 10 acres by now.

Taya was looking after the kids, so she wasn't able to help. Kieron and I rounded up the chickens – we couldn't let them run about because there were foxes around. We shut them in the barn for safe keeping until I could repair the chicken coop. Then I'd be able to secure the cows' field and let them back in there.

**But first, I had some ploughing to do!**

By the time I got to my tractor, the entire morning had been wasted. I could see some clouds on the horizon coming our way. And sunset would be around 5 p.m. **I only had a few hours.** I needed to make it count! If I got in, say, four solid hours in the tractor, I could do two fields, I reckoned. But there wasn't a moment to lose.

I reached down to the ignition switch and then stopped.

'Now,' I said. **'Where have I put the keys?'**

# CHAPTER 9

## THE PIGS

I love pigs. Maybe not so much as cows, but in the Kaleb Scale of Best Animals, they even come above chickens. And believe me, that is really saying something, because chickens (also known as dinosaurs in our house) are **FANTASTIC!**

Here are some interesting facts about pigs that might help explain what's so great about them:

## 1.   Pigs don't sweat

Unlike humans and most other animals, pigs don't have sweat glands. If they want to cool down, they roll around in cold mud.

## 2.   Pigs are athletes!

Maybe they don't look like the fittest of animals, but they can run at speeds of up to 17 kilometres per hour! That's how Bruce had got away from me. In hot countries, wild pigs like to go swimming in the sea to keep cool (and have fun!). They are also good at weightlifting, as Bruce proved when he lifted the heavy gate off its hinges.

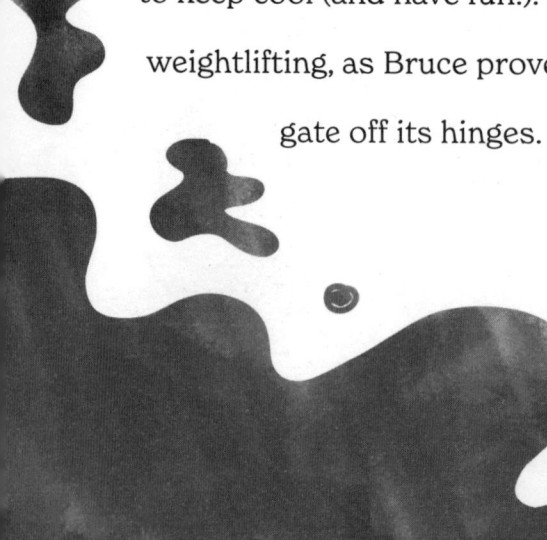

## 3. Pigs are very clean animals

Even though people say a dirty
room is 'like a pigsty', pigs are actually
very clean animals if given the chance. They have
a reputation for being dirty and rolling around in
their own poo, but that's not fair. That only happens
if they're kept in small enclosures. When they've got
a decent amount of space to run about in, like on my
farm, they insist on only the freshest, finest mud to roll
around in.

## 4. Pigs have their own personalities

Just like humans, each pig is different. Some pigs are more active and curious, whereas others are lazy and shy. One of my favourite sows, Hazel, is very sweet and friendly, whilst Bruce is a complete pain in the backside. They have different tastes in food too. One pig might love apples, another might prefer potatoes. Most pigs LOVE a belly rub, just like dogs!

## 5. Pigs can talk!

Pigs talk to each other (and to me) using different grunts and squeals. Mummy pigs have special calls for their piglets. Scientists say that pigs have twenty different words (or sounds) they use to talk to each other. And get this, mother pigs sing to their babies when they feed!

## 6.   Pigs are social

Like a lot of animals, pigs like to be in groups and get sad when they are kept apart from the herd. They make friends with each other and also their humans! When it's cold, they snuggle up with each for warmth and comfort.

## 7.   Pigs are REALLY good at smelling

I don't mean they are very smelly. A pig's strongest sense is their smell. They use their snout to search for food, and for telling each other apart. When I go to feed them in the morning, they smell me long before they see me (and yes, I have had a shower!).

Their sense of smell is around 2,000 times more sensitive than a human's! In some countries, pigs are used to sniff out a special type of fungus called a truffle, which grows underground.

## 8. Pigs have excellent memories

Pigs in the wild can remember places where food can be found. They're good at remembering directions so they can find their way home, and they're very good at recognising and remembering different humans and other pigs. Much better than me, in fact. I'm terrible at remembering people's names.

## 9. Pigs are smarter than dogs

Don't tell Alfie, but pigs are among the smartest animals in the world. They can play games, use tools, recognise their own name and learn basic commands and tricks. Though I have to say, MY pigs only tend to respond to the command, 'Come and get some food'. And their only trick is to roll around in the mud, grunting like crazy.

## 10. My friend Jeremy is actually quite a good pig farmer.

# Don't tell him I said that.

I'm not sure Bruce had quite got the memo about all of the above. He didn't seem particularly bothered about being separated from his herd, for a start, and if he could remember the directions home, he didn't seem interested in following them.

I was a little bit glum after my latest failure to capture Bruce, but I pulled on my wellies and got on with things.

You see, I don't believe in failure. Because if you try something and it doesn't work out, then you've still **GAINED** something by **LEARNING** from it. Maybe what you learned is, **'I'd better not do that again!'** like Oscar did when he got a throat infection after licking the gate. But whatever it is you learned, you're further along than you were.

And I'm sorry to keep banging on about this, but this is why sheep aren't ruling the planet right now. They not only **DON'T** learn anything from their mistakes, but they also **KEEP** making the same mistakes over and over and **THEN** they add new ones on top.

So, I didn't feel too bad about my setbacks with Bruce in the veggie patch, or with the Hansel and Gretel plan. I'd learned some things from the experience. One of the things I learned was that Bruce does very large and smelly poos.

And I was already starting to come up with my next

**cunning plan** to capture him. In the meantime, though, there were other pig-related jobs to do.

There's always a lot of maintenance to do on any farm. I'm not bad with a hammer or a saw, but it is frustrating. You want to be spending your time milking a cow, or shearing a sheep, or collecting eggs, or planting a field with oats. **You know, actual farming?** The work that might mean you get some money coming in for a change instead of going out.

Let's say you need to replace a section of fence. You have to go to the timber-yard and buy some planks. Then you have to go to the hardware store and buy some nails. Then you have to get the tractor out (I don't mind this bit, to be fair) and dig some holes, then put the posts in, then nail the planks to the posts. Then you need to go to the grocery store to buy some frozen peas to put on your thumb because you whacked it with a hammer. It all takes ages and costs loads. A good rule of thumb when working out how much something is going to cost is to think of a number, then double it.

And in the end, all you've got is a slightly nicer, newer fence than you had before.

**Oh, and a bruised thumb.**

Do you see what I mean? You're not actually getting anywhere. You're not moving **FORWARD**. You're working just to stay where you are.

The rain had come back **AGAIN** and Kieron and I reluctantly decided we had to take a break from harvesting for a few days. But at least this gave us the opportunity to get some serious hammering done.

First, we replaced the fence on the field the cows had got out of recently.

Then we rebuilt the chicken houses and replaced the chicken wire fence around the coop. We made it extra strong so that it wouldn't keep out just foxes, but any cows trying to get through too.

**And finally came the BIGGEST job of all.**

We had to build a new pen for Bruce. Not that we'd caught him yet, mind. Taya reckoned she'd seen him up on his hill a couple of days earlier, but other than that he was keeping a low profile. Or as low a profile as a 250 kg boar can keep.

But when we did catch him, we knew we'd need something strong enough that he could never break out again. **A maximum-security facility.**

The sows watched us with interest as we reinforced the existing fences around the pen. We used metal posts embedded in concrete.

The gate I'd bought (at great expense) was made of heavy iron. We had to use the tractor to lift it and slot it into the brackets. There was no way Bruce would be smashing or lifting that gate.

**Oscar was a big help.** Kieron told him we were training him up as a gopher.

'What's a gopher?' he asked.

'Someone who'll go for this and go for that,' Kieron said. 'Now, go for that hammer and pass it to me.'

When we'd finished. We stepped back and admired our handiwork.

'Not bad,' Kieron said.

'There's no animal could break out of there,' I said. 'Not even a bull.'

'Not even an elephant,' Oscar added.

'Not even a whale,' I said. It was unlikely there would be a whale in the Chadlington area, but if one ever did come by, we could definitely have held her captive in our new maximum-security facility.

'It's like Fort Knox,' Kieron replied.

'What's that?' Oscar asked.

'It's a big fort in America where they keep all their gold. No one can break in or out.'

From then on, that was what we called Bruce's pig pen. Fort Knox.

'Still not much use if we can't catch him,' Kieron said.

'Don't worry,' I said. 'I have a **BRILLIANT** plan.'

But the plan had to wait. Because there were other, more urgent pig-related jobs to do.

Everyone on a farm has a job. Well, we all have lots of jobs, but there's always one job that everyone is particularly good at. I'm the best at driving tractors, for example. Alfie is an expert tennis ball protector. Kieron is good with handling cows, the kids are among the top egg collectors in the country, and Taya's job? Well, Taya is the expert when it comes to baby animals, helping

the mums give birth, looking after the lambs or the chicks or the calves when they are taking their first unsteady steps in this bright new world. I'm not nearly so good. I'm too impatient, my fingers are too fat and clumsy.

**Taya is a brilliant mum and a really great farmer.**

Our sows tend to have two litters of piglets each year, in the spring and again in the autumn. They usually have **TEN piglets** in each litter, so that really adds up. After a while we're **swimming in piglets**, so we sell some of them to other farms when they're old enough.

But that means we get to hang on to the piglets when they're at their ABSOLUTE cutest! Sure, kittens are sweet and puppies are adorable, but there's nothing cuter than a bunch of fat little piglets charging about, oinking as they go. From time to time, they get the **zoomies**, as we call it, and just go **absolutely**

# BANANAS racing around the pen, bashing into

each other or their mum or the fence. It's great to see because it means they're **healthy** and **happy**.

Oscar loves the piglets and has been known to ride one of them from time to time. **Just like me with Chug!**

At the time Bruce was off on his adventures around the area, one of his wives, Hazel, was farrowing, which means she was having her babies. A rough rule of thumb is that pigs are pregnant for three months, three weeks and three days. The babies usually arrive bang on time. We knew it could happen any day.

'We have a good idea what day they'll arrive,' Taya was telling Oscar that morning. 'But not the exact time.'

'We know exactly what time they're going to arrive,' I said, grumpily. 'At two in the morning, because that's the time everything kicks off around here.'

**Turns out I was wrong.** Hazel began farrowing at three in the morning, giving me a whole extra hour in bed. So that was something. Like I said, Taya is the expert at baby time, but pigs are big and stubborn, so she needed me there as chief pig-shover.

So we pulled on our wellies and headed down to the barn.

I popped into the hen enclosure on the way and shouted **BOO** at Jeff to wake him up.

The first piglet had already popped out by the time we got there, so Taya gave it a brisk rub down with some hay and helped it to find a teat to suckle on. Hazel was lying on her side, breathing heavily. Sometimes a farrowing sow will stand up and walk around then flop down again, and you have to be careful to make sure they don't sit down on their babies and squash them!

We don't usually give the pigs names. Apart from Bruce the Boar, that is, and Hazel. When it comes to the piglets, there are so many of them it's impossible to keep track of who is who anyway, and it's easier to say goodbye if they don't have names. They're not pets, remember?

Over the next couple of hours, Hazel popped out piglets at regular intervals. By 5 a.m. we had three boys and two girls.

'This is too easy,' I said. 'Maybe I can go back to bed?'

'You're not going anywhere,' Taya replied.

To pass the time, I sang 'This Little Piggy' with the five piglets we had so far. Taya asked me to stop after a while because she said my singing was putting Hazel off.

It took another half an hour for the next two piglets to come out, both boys, squealing and wriggly, fat and pink.

Then there were two more girls and we had nine! Not quite enough for a football team.

'If we get two more, I'll name them all after the Manchester United team that won last year's FA Cup,' I told Taya. She rolled her eyes.

I pointed to one of the bigger boys. 'This one's called **Marcus Rasherford.** Get it?'

The first rays of sunlight were starting to appear in the sky over the yard, reflected off the clouds, as pink as a piglet. **I sighed happily.** Despite the lack of sleep, it felt good. **I felt alive.** I felt like farming was important, that I was good at it, that I was doing a good thing. We'd brought nine more lives into the world this morning. Nine healthy, squealing, cute-as-a-button piglets greedily guzzling their mother's milk. They would be doing zoomies in a few weeks.

'There's one more piglet in there,' Taya said. 'But it's not moving.'

'Oh,' I said. 'Oh dear.'

And that's the thing about farming. Just like in the wild, some animals don't survive. No matter what you do, how careful you are, some animals just don't make it. The world can be a cruel place sometimes. Even in our quiet little barn on a beautiful autumn morning.

The final piglet was born after another half an hour, and as Taya had thought, it wasn't moving. It was tiny, the runt of the litter for sure. A boy. Whilst all its brothers and sisters were slurping down creamy milk from their mum's teats, the poor little thing just lay still in the straw.

'It's a real shame,' I said, laying a hand on Taya's shoulder.

Taya gave me a look. 'One more try,' she said. 'We can't give up now.'

We knelt over the little piglet, leaned down and started massaging its belly.

'Sometimes you can get them breathing again,' I said.

Taya made sure the sow had plenty of milk to drink. She'd need to keep up her strength. The other fat little piglets were happily drinking milk. Some of them already had full bellies and had rolled away to sleep.

'He's breathing,' I said.

Taya grinned. We couldn't believe it. The little runt was breathing, tiny little breaths. His eyes were closed tightly and he was lying perfectly still. Except not quite. His little chest was rising, oh so gently.

**'That's amazing!'** I said.

I've been a farmer my whole life and I thought I knew pretty much everything there was to know about this funny old business. But I learned something that morning. That caring for animals isn't just building pens and fencing fields and getting up early for milking. It's not just about making money either. It's more than that. It's about caring and loving and protecting. And doing your best for your animals, or your crops.

We're just a small patch of land in a small country on a small planet. The piglet was just a runt, in a litter that was plenty big enough. In a way, the life of one tiny piglet didn't matter. But to us, in that moment, that little piglet was the most important thing in the universe.

## We called the runt Jeremy.

# CHAPTER 10

## THE HARVEST

One of the best days out you'll ever have is at an agricultural show. They are **BRILLIANT!** You'll see more than if you go to the cinema, you'll have more fun than at the circus and you'll see more animals than in the zoo. And you can even buy some and take them home! As long as you have enough space in your garden. Don't get too excited and buy a cow to take back to your high-rise apartment in the city.

That's not going to work out.

Taya and I took the kids to a show recently. I wasn't really in the market to buy any new animals or farm machinery, but it doesn't hurt to look. And there are loads of stalls selling yummy homemade cheese and meat and chocolates and whatnot, and they give you samples for free.

Oscar and I ate so much cheese we were nearly sick.

It was there that I first had my **BRILLIANT** idea for how to catch Bruce the Boar.

OK, Taya has just reminded me that it was actually Oscar's idea, really. But I improved it.

We spent a long time looking at the cows and the pigs that were for sale. I walked straight past the sheep pens without making eye contact. But then we came face to face with a farmer who had a large Cotswold sheep on a lead. He was showing it off to a few people and despite myself, I stopped to watch. Cotswolds are a lovely sheep, I have to admit – they have very long wool. *Maybe I could get some Cotswolds*, I suddenly found myself thinking. Maybe I'd get a bit more for the wool since there was more of it, and who knows, maybe they were a bit easier to handle. This one certainly looked calm and sensible.

Anyway, then someone stepped up towards the handler and his Cotswold to have a closer look and the sheep suddenly got a fright and took off like a rocket! The handler's hand was looped through the lead and before you could say Jack Robinson he was pulled off his feet and was getting dragged along the grass.

'That's one strong sheep,' Taya said, admiringly, as the Cotswold and her hapless handler barrelled into a trestle table at a cake stall, sending the French fancies and sponge cakes flying.

I shook my head at the chaos. And to think that I'd even for a second considered buying another sheep. I must be mad.

We carried on. I would have wanted to look longer at the chickens, but the others made me hurry up so we could get some candy floss. Oscar ate all his in twelve seconds and this time he **WAS** sick.

After that, we went to look at the farm machinery. I love this part. There are diggers and harvesters and drillers and ploughs and, best of all, they have loads and loads of . . . you guessed it.

**TRACTORS.**

'Look at that one!' Oscar said, admiring a John Deere 8R 410.

'He has a good eye for tractors, I'll give him that,' I said. Taya sighed.

'I used to have a wooden tractor,' I said.

'Really?' Oscar said.

**'Yeah, it wooden go,'** I said. Nobody laughed.

*Just as well I'm a farmer and not a stand-up comedian*, I thought. Or a singer . . .

But it wasn't actually the tractors that helped us with our plan for Bruce. It was the ring feeders. We were talking about Bruce and what we were going to do to catch him.

'We can't throw him into the pen because he's too big and strong,' I explained to Oscar. 'We can't trick him into the pen because he's too smart.'

Oscar nodded wisely. He'd recovered from his candy floss overdose by then.

'So what do I do?' I asked.

'Trap him,' Oscar said, simply.

And then, as I looked at the ring feeder, a light bulb went off in my head.

A ring feeder is a piece of equipment that does exactly what it says on the tin. We farmers are simple folk, and we call things what they are. It's a big ring that you fill with animal feed, then you plonk it down in a field and all the animals come running up and eat themselves silly.

You can use it for any medium to large animal – **pigs**, **sheep**, **cows**, **goats**, **llamas**, err . . . I don't know, probably buffalo? You might need to use something else for **elephants** and **giraffes**. I wouldn't know, having never owned either of them, but maybe one day, when I've bought my farm . . .

There's one other important thing to know about ring feeders. You can move them about with your tractor. You hook the feeder to a front loader on the tractor. (A front loader is the two arms at the front of the tractor attached to a big bucket shovel. It's like a small bulldozer.) Then you lift the front loader and the ring feeder goes up with it. Then you can drive the tractor to a different field and drop the feeder there.

You can also use the front loader to pour more feed into the ring to keep it topped up.

# Tractors are brilliant.

That's right. I got to use the tractor in my plan. OK, Taya, Oscar's plan.

So the next day, I once again found myself roaring up the hill to the little wood where Bruce was hiding out. Taya had started calling it Bruce's Wood. Alfie was beside me, looking serious. He knew there was an important job to do.

**I had three things.** A big sack of apples, overripe and smelling strong, a massive new ring feeder attached to the front loader, and my trusty tractor. Those three things, along with my ingenuity and skill with a tractor, were all we'd need.

I raised the ring up high, then got out of the tractor, telling Alfie to stay put. He had a couple of tennis balls in there to keep an eye on so he wasn't going anywhere.

I emptied the apples into a pile in the field, just a few feet from the last place I'd spotted Bruce. I crunched a few to release that delicious smell. Then I got back in the cab and sat still.

Alfie whined after a few minutes, asking what we were doing. He's not used to me sitting still.

I like to sing in my cab, along with my music playing

at full blast. When I'm there I can sing as well as Elvis Presley, or Ed Sheeran, or The Wurzels. And there's no one to tell me I'm rubbish. But today we had to be quiet. We didn't want to spook Bruce, and a few bars of me singing 'I've Got a Brand New Combine Harvester' was enough to frighten off a whole herd of boar!

**'We're on stakeout,'** I whispered to Alfie. 'You know, like in detective films.' Alfie shrugged and settled down to sleep.

It was warm and cosy in the cab. I could only hear the wind shaking the mostly leafless branches of the woods and the occasional caw of a crow in the distance. It was very peaceful and I thought maybe I could get used to sitting around doing nothing.

I think I must have dropped off for a few moments, and that nearly brought the whole plan crashing down.

Alfie saved the day by barking. I woke with a start and saw Bruce just finishing off the last of the apples.

He looked up in surprise at Alfie's bark and I sensed he was going to bolt.

'**Not so fast,**' I growled and pulled the lever I'd had my hand on all this time.

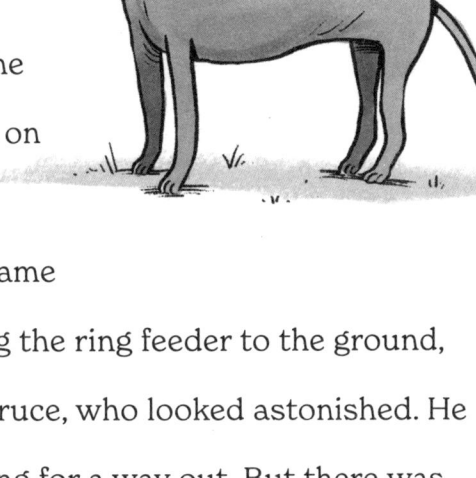

The front loader came down sharp, dropping the ring feeder to the ground, neatly surrounding Bruce, who looked astonished. He spun in a circle, looking for a way out. But there was none.

# We had him now!

I got on the two-way radio and called Kieron. He ran right there.

'**Brilliant!**' Kieron shouted when he saw the captured boar. '**Well done, Kaleb!**'

'It's called a ring for a reason, Brucey,' I said. '**Not so smart now, are you?!**' I laughed like an evil villain in a film. It was such a relief to have finally caught that fugitive.

'So, what now?' Kieron asked, when I'd finally stopped cackling.

'**What?**' I replied.

'So, what now?' Kieron repeated. 'You've got him trapped. But you can't leave him here.'

'I know that,' I snapped. But Kieron had a point. **I hadn't actually thought what I might do with Bruce once he was trapped within the feeder.**

'We need to get him back to Fort Knox,' Kieron went on. 'You see . . .'

'Yes, thank you, Kieron,' I interrupted. 'Be quiet and let me think.'

Bruce grunted noisily and bashed his head into the ring feeder with a great crash. Alfie barked.

'OK,' I said. 'Here's what we do, right. We lift the ring just a little. Not high enough that he can squeeze under it. Then we drive the tractor down the hill right into Fort Knox, then we slam the gate shut.'

'You'll run him over!' Kieron protested.

'Not if I drive really slowly,' I said.

'You've never driven slowly in your life,' he said.

**He had a point.**

'Every day's a school day,' I said. 'Now watch and learn.' I raised the ring a few inches off the ground, then locked it in place. Then I put the tractor into its lowest gear and took my foot a little off the clutch. The tractor engine throbbed and slowly the wheels began to move.

The ring feeder jolted forward and **bashed Bruce on the bum**. He squealed and moved a couple of feet away. The tractor crawled forward and the feeder **bumped his bottom** once more. He spun around and tried to bash the feeder with his head. But it was too big and heavy, especially with a massive great tractor attached to it. Poor old Bruce had no choice but to turn around and carry on walking down the hill.

# 'It's working, it's working!'

I cried triumphantly.

'Great,' Kieron said, walking alongside. 'At this rate we might even get to Fort Knox by Christmas.'

'First I'm driving too fast, now I'm too slow,' I said. 'Make up your mind.'

Kieron walked alongside the feeder, keeping it from swinging back and forward too much. I kept up the slow pace. Kieron was right. It was going to take a long old time to get back home. The autumn sun was setting over the fields to the west. But there wasn't another way.

In the end, it took us nearly two hours to get down the hill and back to the yard. It was completely dark by then. Taya, Oscar and little Willa came out to greet us when we reached the barn.

'Yay!' cried Oscar.

'Woooo!' hollered Willa.

'Your dinner's cold,' said Taya.

I carried on guiding Bruce right into Fort Knox, then dropped the ring feeder. I backed out of the pen, and we shut the door. Then I attached a chain to the ring feeder and used the front loader to lift it up and away, leaving Bruce free to roam around his new home.

**He didn't look happy.** But then Kieron opened the door to the sows' huts and all Bruce's mad little children came running out, clustering around him, sniffing their old man, asking him where he'd been and had he brought them anything?

At first, he seemed astonished to see all his kids there. But then he flopped down and started scratching his back on the rough stones of the pen while his kids went completely bonkers, racing around and piling on top of him.

Bruce was back home with his family, where he belonged. And he looked like he might be OK with it.

I gave my own little family a hug. Then we went in for tea.

# EPILOGUE

## THE END IS ALSO THE BEGINNING

I'm writing this a week before Christmas. In the dead
of winter. The publishing
people said they needed the
book before Christmas,
and just like Santa Claus,
I'm not one to miss a
deadline.

The days are short, gloomy and cold. The nights are long and frosty. This is the quietest time on the farms around here. There are still jobs to do, of course – the cows still need to be milked, the pigs must be fed. The sheep still need to escape and run off in the direction of danger. Jeff still needs to scream at us at four every morning. Alfie still needs to watch his collection of balls very carefully. I still need to find my tractor keys.

Maybe I could ask Santa for a spare set?

But there are no animals being born at this time of the year. The spring piglets and the calves have been sold. The turkeys have finished their holiday and left. The crops have all been harvested and sold to people who are looking forward to eating them with their Christmas dinner. Even the sprouts, yuk.

The fields lie still and quiet. This time of year feels like the end of everything. But it isn't. It's actually the beginning. Because as we're eating chocolates and watching the King's speech or a Christmas film on the telly, things are stirring. While we're inside warm and happy and laughing at stupid cracker jokes, buds are appearing on the trees and hedgerows.

While we're singing along with Christmas songs on the radio and hanging up a stocking for Father Christmas, snowdrops and daffodil bulbs are sprouting green shoots which push up towards the dim sunlight.

Many of the sheep have little ones growing in their bellies. Some of the sows too. The farmers I work for are talking to me about what they're going to grow next year and ordering the seed. We'll think about how many new cows we want. How many lambs and piglets we're hoping for. How we can make some money from milk and wool for a change! And maybe I might have a little look at the tractor catalogue . . .

Soon it'll be January, and time to get back in the tractor to break up the fields with the heavy plough. I might sing a couple of songs while I'm doing it. We'll probably need to fix some fences too and install a new water tank for the pigs. Then it'll be spreading fertiliser on the fields (from last year's poo).

Then in February the lambs come. Then it's the turn of the piglets. In March we'll do most of the planting (once it stops raining, that is). The sun will be starting to warm the soil then, the tree buds will be bursting open and the margins will be sprouting with the shoots of wildflowers. Alfie will lose a tennis ball in the weeds and I'll buy him a new one.

In April we plant potatoes and the last of the lambs arrive. The leaves will be out on the trees and the birds will be cheeping and tweeting in the hedgerows. The cows will have their calves. Then the sheep will probably escape.

In May the fruit trees will be in full bloom, blossom floating around on the breeze. Maybe Manchester United will win the FA Cup again!

In June we'll shear the sheep (if we can find them). I might get myself shorn down at Jojo's at the same time, as a treat. June is also the time we'll make hay to keep the animals fed for next winter. We'll be collecting the animals' poo and letting it rot down nicely. Mmmm.

In July we might go to an agricultural show and buy some new animals (not sheep), some new machinery and maybe a new tractor! This is the time the soft berries are ripe for picking – cherries, raspberries, strawberries and blueberries. The wild brambles in the hedgerows will be bursting with blackberries and the birds will be feeding on them like crazy.

And soon enough September will come around. I'll go outside and shout at the rain clouds. Once they're gone, we can harvest the barley, then the oats, the wheat and finally the potatoes. We'll make apple juice and pear cider; we'll have another bunch of crazy piglets running zoomies around their pen. The town will hold a harvest festival and we'll all get to decorate our tractors and ride them down the high street.

The sheep will escape again.

In October we'll be ploughing and cultivating to get the fields ready for the winter crops. We'll pick pumpkins, feed most to the pigs and make jack-o-lanterns with the rest.

Might get a new haircut too. Maybe my maddest haircut yet, to scare the kids at Hallowe'en.

In November we'll bring the animals indoors to keep them cosy and warm during the winter. This is when we plant spring bulbs and new trees. And then it's December again and mostly farm maintenance and tending to the livestock. Some farms will be harvesting their winter crops like cauliflower, beetroot, swede, parsnips, leeks and sprouts. The trees will have lost all their leaves, we'll wave goodbye to the turkeys and it'll be time to put the Christmas tree up again.

Maybe next year I'll ask Santa to bring me a new rooster, one who doesn't wake me up at four every morning!

It's hard work being a farmer, and the work never stops. There's always something to do, whatever time of year it is. But we do it because we love it, and because we think that it's important to put good quality food on people's plates – not just at Christmas, but throughout the year.

Sometimes I wonder if I wouldn't have been better off just sticking with chickens. If I just had to worry about raising chickens and selling eggs, my life would be a lot simpler, that's for sure.

And I might have more money!

But I know I wouldn't have been happy. That's why I went back to school, and to college. So I could do more. Experience more. Live more. Growth as a person

only comes when you're learning something by DOING something. I decided I wanted to know more about cows, learn more about pigs, even find out that I hated sheep. Those experiences made me who I am. My life isn't perfect. But it's not far off.

One day, when I walk out into the fields of my own farm, with my kids on either side of me, and together we decide what we're going to plant that year – well, then I can truly say that I'm living my dreams.

But always remember, dreams don't work unless you do.

# AUTHOR BIO

Kaleb Cooper is a farming contractor from Oxfordshire who plays a central advisory role to Jeremy Clarkson in the hit Prime Video series *Clarkson's Farm*. Born in July 1998, he grew up in the Cotswolds and has been working in farming since he was at school. He studied agriculture at Moreton Morrell College and likes collecting tractors and cars, but is not so keen on sheep. His first book, *The World According to Kaleb*, was an instant *Sunday Times* bestseller. He lives in Chipping Norton with his young family and doesn't like to leave the county. This book is his first for all his young farming fans.

# IF YOU LIKED THIS, WHY NOT TRY . . .

ANIMAL ALL-STARS

INCREDIBLE FACTS, STATS AND STORIES FROM THE GREATEST RECORD-BREAKERS IN THE ANIMAL WORLD

CLARE BALDING

ILLUSTRATED BY THE BOY FITZ HAMMOND

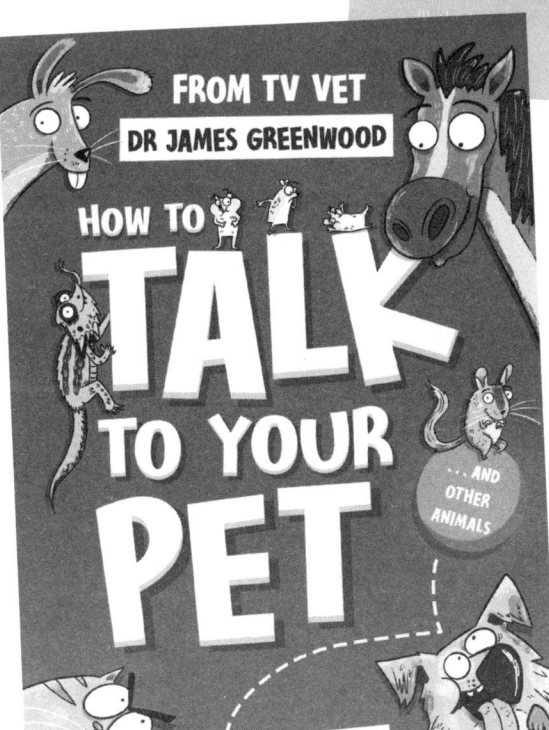